DEEPENING
LIFE
TOGETHER

EPHESIANS

LIFE TOGETHER

BakerBooks
a division of Baker Publishing Group
Grand Rapids, Michigan

© 2009 by Lifetogether Publishing

Published by Baker Books
a division of Baker Publishing Group
P.O. Box 6287, Grand Rapids, MI 49516-6287
www.bakerbooks.com

Printed in the United States of America

Library of Congress Cataloging-in-Publication Data
Ephesians / [editors, Mark L. Strauss, Teresa Haymaker].
    p. cm. — (Deepening life together)
    Includes bibliographical references.
    ISBN 978-0-8010-6845-4 (pbk.)
    1. Bible. N.T. Ephesians—Textbooks. 2. Bible. N.T. Ephesians—Study and teaching.
I. Strauss, Mark L. II. Haymaker, Teresa.
BS2695.55.E63 2009
227'.50071—dc22   2009014248

CONTENTS

Contents

ACKNOWLEDGMENTS

The *Deepening Life Together: Ephesians* Small Group Video Bible Study has come together through the efforts of many at Baker Publishing Group, Lifetogether Publishing, and Lamplighter Media for which we express our heartfelt thanks.

Executive Producer	John Nill
Producer and Director	Sue Doc Ross
Editors	Mark L. Strauss (Scholar), Teresa Haymaker
Curriculum Development	Brett Eastman, Lori Hensley, Sue Doc Ross, Stephanie French, Teresa Haymaker, Virgil Hurley, Mark L. Strauss, Karen Lee-Thorp
Video Production	Chris Balish, Rodney Bissell, Nick Calabrese, Sebastian Hoppe Fuentes, Josh Greene, Patrick Griffin, Teresa Haymaker, Oziel Jabin Ibarra, Natali Ibarra, Janae Janik, Keith Sorrell, Lance Tracy
Teachers and Scholars	Clint Arnold, Lynn Cohick, Andrew Hill, Moyer Hubbard, Jon Laansma, Mike Meeks, Nick Perrin, Mark Strauss
Baker Publishing Group	Jack Kuhatschek

Special thanks to DeLisa Ivy, Bethel Seminary, Talbot School of Theology, Wheaton College

Clips from The JESUS Film are copyright © 1995–2009 The JESUS Film Project®. A ministry of Campus Crusade for Christ International®.

Interior icons by Tom Clark

READ ME FIRST

Most people want to live a healthy, balanced spiritual life, but few achieve this by themselves. And most small groups struggle to balance all of God's purposes in their meetings. Groups tend to overemphasize one of the five purposes, perhaps fellowship or discipleship. Rarely is there a healthy balance that includes evangelism, ministry, and worship. That's why we've included all of these elements in this study so you can live a healthy, balanced spiritual life over time.

A typical group session will include the following:

Memory Verses

For each session we have provided a memory verse that emphasizes an important truth from the session. This is an optional exercise, but we believe that memorizing Scripture can be a vital part of filling our minds with God's Word. We encourage you to give this important habit a try.

 ### CONNECTING *with God's Family (Fellowship)*

The foundation for spiritual growth is an intimate connection with God and his family. A few people who really know you and who earn your trust provide a place to experience the life Jesus invites you to live. This section of each session typically offers you two activities. You can get to know your whole group by using the icebreaker question, and/or you can check in with one or two group members—your spiritual partner(s)—for a deeper connection and encouragement in your spiritual journey.

DVD TEACHING SEGMENT. A *Deepening Life Together: Ephesians* Video Teaching DVD companion to this study guide is available. For each study session, the DVD contains a lesson taught by Mike Meeks. If you are using the DVD, you will view the teaching segment after your *Connecting* discussion and before your group discussion time (the *Growing* section). At the end of each session in this study guide, you will find space for your notes on the teaching segment.

GROWING *to Be Like Christ (Discipleship)*

Here is where you come face-to-face with Scripture. In core passages you'll explore what the Bible teaches about the topic of the study. The focus won't be on accumulating information but on how we should live in light of the Word of God. We want to help you apply the Scriptures practically, creatively, and from your heart as well as your head. At the end of the day, allowing the timeless truths from God's Word to transform our lives in Christ is our greatest aim.

DEVELOPING *Your Gifts to Serve Others (Ministry)*

Jesus trained his disciples to discover and develop their gifts to serve others. And God has designed each of us uniquely to serve him in a way no other person can. This section will help you discover and use your God-given design. It will also encourage your group to discover your unique design as a community. In this study, you'll put into practice what you've learned in the Bible study by taking a step to serve others. These simple steps will take your group on a faith journey that could change your lives forever.

SHARING *Your Life Mission Every Day (Evangelism)*

Many people skip over this aspect of the Christian life because it's scary, relationally awkward, or simply too much work for their busy schedules. But Jesus wanted all of his disciples to help outsiders connect with him, to know him personally. This doesn't mean preaching on street corners. It could mean welcoming a few newcomers into your group, hosting a short-term group in your home, or walking through this study with a friend. In this study, you'll have an opportunity to go beyond Bible study to biblical living.

SURRENDERING *Your Life for God's Pleasure (Worship)*

God is most pleased by a heart that is fully his. Each group session will give you a chance to surrender your heart to God in prayer and worship. You may read a psalm together, share a page in your journal, or sing a song to close your meeting. If you have never prayed aloud in a group before, no one will pressure you. Instead, you'll experience the support of others who are praying for you.

Study Notes

This section provides background notes on the Bible passage(s) you examine in the *Growing* section. You may want to refer to these notes during your group meeting or as a reference for those doing additional study.

For Deeper Study (Optional)

If you want to dig deeper into more Bible passages about the topic at hand, we've provided additional passages and questions. Your group may choose to do study homework ahead of each meeting in order to cover more biblical material. Or you as an individual may choose to study the *For Deeper Study* on your own. If you prefer not to do study homework, the *Growing* section will provide you with plenty to discuss within the group. These options allow individuals or the whole group to go deeper in their study, while still accommodating those who can't do homework or are new to your group.

You can record your discoveries in your journal. We encourage you to read some of your insights to a friend (spiritual partner) for accountability and support. Spiritual partners may check in each week over the phone, through e-mail, or at the beginning of the group meeting.

Reflections

On the *Reflections* pages we provide Scriptures to read and reflect on between group meetings. We suggest you use this section to seek God at home throughout the week. This time at home should begin and end with prayer. Don't get in a hurry; take enough time to hear God's direction.

Subgroup for Discussion and Prayer

If your group is large (more than seven people), we encourage you to separate into groups of two to four for discussion and prayer. This is to encourage greater participation and deeper discussion.

INTRODUCTION

Welcome to the *Deepening Life Together* Bible study on *Ephesians*. As we live this Bible study experience together, we will unpack principles from God's Word that reveal God's divine purpose and plan of bringing redemption to his people and the outworking of that purpose in the life of the believer.

The letter to the Ephesians covers a vast amount of doctrine and practice in a very short space. It is one of four "prison letters" (Ephesians, Philippians, Colossians, and Philemon) probably written during Paul's first Roman imprisonment, around AD 60 (see Acts 28:3–31).

This journey through the book of Ephesians will connect you with our loving and faithful God and with other believers. For some of you, this might be the first time you've connected in a small group community. We want you to know that God cares about you and your spiritual growth. As you prayerfully respond to the principles you learn in this study, God will move you to a deeper level of commitment and intimacy with himself, as well as with those in your small group.

We at Baker Books and Lifetogether Publishing look forward to hearing the stories of how God changes you from the inside out during this small group experience. We pray God blesses you with all he has planned for you through this journey together.

> For the LORD is good and his love endures forever;
> his faithfulness continues through all generations.
>
> Psalm 100:5 (NIV)

AN ALMIGHTY GOD, A GLORIOUS CHURCH

Memory Verse: Praise be to the God and Father of our Lord Jesus Christ, who has blessed us in the heavenly realms with every spiritual blessing in Christ (Eph. 1:3 NIV).

A principal claim of the Internet is information on demand. One can look up information on just about any topic, any time of the day or night. But having information available doesn't assure understanding; we must take the information in, digest it, question it, and accept it before it can be of any value to us.

The same applies to Scripture; only when we read and understand it deeply and thoroughly will we begin to understand it to the point that we begin to question the way we live. Just knowing that we have been "blessed . . . in the heavenly realms with every spiritual blessing" (Eph. 1:3) should energize our gratitude and boost our self-esteem, but knowledge of this alone will not help us attain it.

In Ephesians chapter 1, Paul reveals God's eternal purpose and plan for every believer. God has chosen and saved each of us for redemption and secured for us a promised inheritance. Together we will embrace the reality of God's perfect plan and allow it to motivate us to trust him in every area of life, with his purpose becoming our life's mission.

Connecting

Begin your group time with prayer. Ask God to open your hearts to receive his Word through this Bible study and for the courage to change as he challenges you in the weeks to come.

Deeper relationships happen when we take the time to keep in touch with one another. As you begin, pass around a copy of the *Small Group Roster*, a sheet of paper, or one of you pass your study guide, opened to the *Small Group Roster*. When the roster gets to you, write down your contact information, including the best time and method for contacting you. Then, someone volunteer to make copies or type up a list with everyone's information and e-mail it to the group this week.

1. Begin this first session by introducing yourselves. Include your name, what you do for a living, and what you do for fun. You may also include whether or not you are married, how long you have been married, how many children you have and their ages. Also share what brought you to this small group study of Ephesians and what you expect to learn during the next seven sessions.

2. Whether your group is new or ongoing, it's always important to reflect on and review your group values together. In the *Appendix* is a *Small Group Agreement* with the values we've found most useful in sustaining healthy, balanced groups. We recommend that you review these values and choose one or two—values you haven't previously focused on or have room to grow in—to emphasize during this study. Choose values that will take your group to the next stage of intimacy and spiritual health. Discuss how you will implement these values in your small group.

3. What would you say is God's purpose for your life, as you understand it now? If you don't know, make a guess.

Growing

After greeting the church at Ephesus, Paul gives praise to God as he reveals to his readers God's eternal purpose and plan for every believer.

Please read Ephesians 1.

4. Paul customarily begins his letters with a greeting. See the *Study Notes* for more insight into Paul. Reread Ephesians 1:1–2. What do you think Paul means to communicate by addressing his readers as "God's holy people" and "the faithful in Christ Jesus"?

5. In Ephesians 1:3–14, Paul gives praise to God for the spiritual blessings that we have received in Christ. The chart below outlines some of these. Read them aloud with their corresponding verse and discuss how each of these is integral to God's master plan for salvation.

In Christ I am . . . (v. 3a)	Scripture: Praise be to the God and Father of our Lord Jesus Christ . . .
Blessed (v. 3b)	. . . who has blessed us in the heavenly realms with every spiritual blessing in Christ.
Chosen (v. 4)	For he chose us in him before the creation of the world to be holy and blameless in his sight. In love . . .
Predestined (v. 5)	. . . he predestined us . . . (see *Study Notes* for insight)
Adopted (v. 5)	. . . to be adopted as his sons through Jesus Christ, in accordance with his pleasure and will . . .
Accepted (v. 6)	. . . to the praise of his glorious grace, which he has freely given us in the One he loves.
Redeemed (v. 7)	In him we have redemption through his blood . . . (see *Study Notes* for insight)
Forgiven (v. 7)	. . . the forgiveness of sins, in accordance with the riches of God's grace . . .

Enlightened (vv. 8–9)	. . . that he lavished on us with all wisdom and understanding. And he made known to us the mystery of his will according to his good pleasure, which he purposed in Christ . . .
Sealed (v. 13)	And you also were included in Christ when you heard the word of truth, the gospel of your salvation. Having believed, you were marked in him with a seal, the promised Holy Spirit . . .
Assured (v. 14)	. . . who is a deposit guaranteeing our inheritance until the redemption of those who are God's possession—to the praise of his glory.

6. Read Ephesians 1:4–7. What do we learn from these verses about God's purpose for choosing us to be adopted as his sons (and daughters)?

How does it feel to know that God chose you before the creation of the world?

7. How does one receive redemption and forgiveness of sins according to verse 7? (See the *Study Notes* for a definition of redemption.)

What further insight does Peter give into our redemption in 1 Peter 1:18–21?

8. Read Ephesians 1:8–10. What is the significance of saying God has "lavished" his grace on us?

What is the "mystery" spoken of in verse 9? See the *Study Notes* for help understanding the mystery.

9. What is the Holy Spirit's role in a believer's life according to Ephesians 1:13–14?

How does God's blessing of the Holy Spirit serve as a deposit guaranteeing our inheritance (or pledge of our inheritance)?

10. For what specifically does Paul pray in verse 17?

How does the Spirit's wisdom help us to know God better?

11. What does Paul mean by the "eyes of your heart" in verse 18? (See the *Study Notes* for help.)

Why do you think spiritual enlightenment is necessary in order for believers to fully comprehend the hope to which they were called?

12. Read Paul's description of the power of God in Ephesians 1:18–23. How does this power become accessible to us?

How can God's power empower you in your daily life as you walk with Jesus?

In this first chapter of Paul's letter to the church at Ephesus, Paul reveals to his readers God's eternal purpose and plan for the church. According to this plan, God chose and saved his people for redemption that is available through the sacrificial death of Jesus Christ and secures for the redeemed a promised inheritance. It is Paul's earnest prayer for the Ephesian Christians, and all Christians, that they may fully realize God's purpose and power in their lives.

Developing

God created us to serve him and has given every believer special gifts to be used in service as the Holy Spirit leads. The first step in developing the gifts that God has given each of us is to deepen our relationship with him through prayer, reflection, and meditation on his Word. Through these disciplines, we learn how to hear his voice and submit to the leading of the Holy Spirit.

13. Developing our ability to serve God according to the leading of the Holy Spirit requires that we make time to let God speak to us daily. Which of the following next steps toward this goal are you willing to take for the next few weeks?

☐ **Prayer.** Commit to connecting with God daily through personal prayer. It's important to separate yourself from the distractions in your life so you can really focus on communicating with God. Some people find it helpful to write out their prayers in a journal.

☐ **Reflection.** At the end of each session, you'll find *Reflections* Scriptures that specifically relate to the topic of our study for the session. These are provided to give you an opportunity for reading a short Bible passage five days a week during the course of this study. Write down your insights on what you read each day in the space provided. On the sixth day, summarize what God has shown you throughout the week.

☐ **Meditation.** Psalm 119:11 says, "I have hidden your word in my heart that I might not sin against you" (NIV). Meditation is focused attention on the Word of God and is a great way to internalize God's Word more deeply. One way to do this is to write a portion of Scripture on a card and tape it somewhere where you're sure to see it often, such as your bathroom mirror, car's dashboard, or the kitchen table. Think about it as you get dressed in the morning, when you sit at red lights, or while you're eating a meal. Reflect on what God is saying to you through his words. Consider using the passages provided in the *Reflections* pages in each session. As you meditate upon these Scriptures, you will notice them beginning to take up residence in your heart and mind.

 ## Sharing

Jesus lived and died so that mankind might come to know him and be reconciled to God through him. His final words before his ascension recorded in Acts 1:8 were, "You will receive power when the Holy Spirit comes on you; and you will be my witnesses in Jerusalem, and in all Judea and Samaria, and to the ends of the earth" (NIV). Through the Holy Spirit, we are empowered to be his witnesses to those around us.

14. Jesus wants all of his disciples to help others connect with him, to know him personally. In the weeks to come, you'll be asked

to identify and share with people in your circle of influence who need to know Jesus or need to connect with him through a small group community. With this in mind, as you go about your day-to-day activities this week, pay special attention to the people God has placed in your life. There may be co-workers, family or friends, or other parents at school or sporting events, that you see or talk to on a regular basis. When we meet next time, we'll talk about how to help connect believers to Christian community and begin sharing Jesus with those who don't yet know him.

Surrendering

God wants us to turn our hearts to him. Second Chronicles 16:9 says, "The eyes of the LORD search the whole earth in order to strengthen those whose hearts are fully committed to him" (NLT). Each week you will have a chance to surrender your hearts to God in worship and prayer.

15. Consider some different ways to worship that might fit your group. Following are a few ideas. Spend a few minutes worshiping God together.

    ☐ Have someone use their musical gifts to lead the group in a worship song. You might sing a simple chorus a cappella, with guitar/piano accompaniment, or with a worship CD.

    ☐ Read a passage of Scripture aloud together, making it a time of praise and worship as the words remind you of all God has done for you. Choose a psalm or other favorite verses.

    ☐ Spend a few minutes praising God aloud. You may highlight some of the attributes of God's character or praise him for specific circumstances in your life.

16. Every believer should have a plan for spending time alone with God. Your time with God is personal and reflects who you are in relationship with God. However you choose to spend your time with him, try to allow time for praise, prayer, and

reading of Scripture. *Reflections* are provided at the end of each session for you to use as part of your daily time with God. These will offer reinforcement of the principles you are learning, and develop or strengthen your habit of time alone with God throughout the week.

17. Before you close your group in prayer, answer this question: "How can we pray for you this week?" Write prayer requests on your *Prayer and Praise Report* and commit to praying for each other throughout the week.

Study Notes

Doctrine of Election: The doctrine of election teaches that we are saved only because of God's grace and mercy; as believers we are not saved by our own merit. It focuses on God's purpose or will (1:5, 9, 11), not on ours.

Paul: Paul (known also as Saul) was a Jew from the tribe of Benjamin. He was raised as a strict Pharisee (see below) (Phil. 3:5), grew up in Tarsus, and was educated under a well-known Jewish rabbi, Gamaliel (Acts 22:3). He was also a Roman citizen, a fact that he used to great advantage at times (Acts 22:27–29). As a zealous Jew, Saul considered Christians to be dangerous opponents of Judaism and Jesus to be a false Messiah. He began persecuting the church until, on the road from Jerusalem to Damascus, he was confronted by the resurrected Christ. At that moment Saul realized that the one he had been persecuting was God's Messiah, the Savior of the world, and he devoted the rest of his life to serving him. Saul the persecutor became Paul the apostle of Jesus Christ.

Pharisees: The Pharisees were a religious party within Judaism who strictly kept the law of Moses and the unwritten "tradition of the elders."

Mystery: The term "mystery," as used by Paul, means something unknown in ages past but now revealed to the people of God. The book of Ephesians is an exposition of God's mystery about Christ. The first chapter is largely an expression of divine purpose. Chapter 2 shows God working out the mystery through his grace. Chapter 3 says the mystery is divinely revealed through Christ and associated with God's divine wisdom (3:9). What was not previously known was that all things will be brought into right relationship with Christ. In the meantime God is working out his mystery in the church, which is composed of all people in one body, Jews and Gentiles alike.

Heavenly Realms (Places): The phrases *heavenly realms* or *heavenly places* occur five times in Ephesians (1:3, 20; 2:6; 3:10; 6:12). It refers to the domain beyond the material world where the ultimate conflict between good and evil takes place. This conflict continues but has already been won by Christ's death and resurrection. This is the realm in which the spiritual blessings were secured for us and then given to us. Our blessings come from heaven, where Christ now lives (1:20), and Christ's gift of the Holy Spirit, the source of all spiritual blessings, came as a result of his ascension to heaven (4:8). Paul is making the point that these blessings are spiritual and not material; thus, they are eternal and not temporal.

Predestined: To predestine is to choose, determine, or set apart beforehand. Believers receive an inheritance from God because they are predestined according to his purpose (Eph. 1:11). God knows before we are born whether we will believe and receive the inheritance.

Redemption: A word occurring nine times in Scripture, and always with the idea of a ransom or price paid. Most occurrences of *apolutrôsis* denote the redemption provided by Christ through his death on the cross. In Ephesians 1:7, it describes something that believers have right now. However, in many occurrences of this word in Scripture, there is a future aspect to redemption, which believers will not experience fully until Jesus returns.

Eyes of Your Heart: When Scripture refers to the *heart* in this context, it covers the whole range of activities that go on within one's inner self, including thinking, grieving, rejoicing, desiring, understanding, and decision making.

For Deeper Study (Optional)

I pray that the eyes of your heart may be enlightened, so that you will know what is the hope of His calling, what are the riches of the glory of His inheritance in the saints (Eph. 1:18 NASB).

1. What does Hebrews 6:4–5 indicate about those who have been enlightened?

2. What does Romans 11:29 say about God's gifts and his call?

3. What do Ephesians 1:7 and Colossians 1:5 indicate about the riches of the glory of his inheritance?

4. How do you think Colossians 1:12 summarizes or clarifies Ephesians 1:18?

Reflections

Reading, reflecting, and meditating on the Word of God is essential to getting to know him deeply. As you read the verses each day, give prayerful consideration to what you learn about God, his Spirit, and his place in your life. Then record your thoughts, insights, or prayer in the *Reflect* section below the verses you read. On the sixth day, record a summary of what you learned over the entire week through this study.

Day 1. Listen, my dear brothers: Has not God chosen those who are poor in the eyes of the world to be rich in faith and to inherit the kingdom he promised those who love him? (James 2:5 NIV).

REFLECT

_____

_____

_____

_____

Day 2. Once you were not a people, but now you are the people of God; once you had not received mercy, but now you have received mercy (1 Peter 2:10 NIV).

REFLECT

_____

_____

_____

_____

Day 3. The Spirit himself testifies with our spirit that we are God's children. Now if we are children, then we are heirs—heirs of God and co-heirs with Christ, if indeed we share in his sufferings in order that we may also share in his glory (Rom. 8:16–17 NIV).

REFLECT

_____

_____

_____

_____

Day 4. So in Christ we who are many form one body, and each member belongs to all the others (Rom. 12:5 NIV).

REFLECT

_____

_____

_____

_____

Day 5. For this reason I too, having heard of the faith in the Lord Jesus which exists among you and your love for all the saints, do not cease giving thanks for you, while making mention of you in my prayers; that the God of our Lord Jesus Christ, the Father of glory, may give to you a spirit of wisdom and of revelation in the knowledge of Him. I pray that the eyes of your heart may be enlightened, so that you will know what is the hope of His calling, what are the riches of the glory of His inheritance in the saints (Eph. 1:15–18 NASB).

REFLECT

_____

_____

_____

_____

Day 6. Use the following space to write any insight God has put in your heart and mind about the things we have looked at in this session and during your *Reflections* time this week.

SUMMARY

_____

_____

_____

_____

BEFORE AND AFTER CHRIST

Memory Verse: But because of his great love for us, God, who is rich in mercy, made us alive with Christ even when we were dead in transgressions—it is by grace you have been saved (Eph. 2:4–5 NIV).

In our high-tech, materialistic, relationship-driven society, many things compete for our devotion. It's easy to be enticed away from God and toward ungodly pursuits. But Christ wants us to keep our focus on him and place all our interests, relationships, desires, possessions, and goals under his control.

When we do this, we are freed from sin's bondage, and brought nearer to God. We become part of God's house. As such, we stand with all God's children, and Christ himself.

Although we were once spiritually dead, we have been made alive in Christ and raised with him to God's right hand. Through salvation, we become part of the new creation, the restoration of all things in Christ.

 **Connecting**

Open your group with prayer, inviting the Holy Spirit to remove any uncertainty that you may have in God's faithfulness to keep his promises.

1. If you have new people joining you for the first time, take a few minutes to briefly introduce yourselves.

2. Healthy small groups rotate leadership. We recommend that you rotate leaders/facilitators on a regular basis. This practice helps to develop every member's ability to shepherd a few people within a safe environment. Even Jesus gave others the opportunity to serve alongside him.

    It's also a good idea to rotate host homes, with the host of each meeting providing the refreshments. Some groups like to let the host lead the meeting each week, while others like to allow one person to host while another person leads.

    The *Small Group Calendar* is a tool for planning who will lead and host each meeting. Take a few minutes to plan leaders and hosts for your remaining meetings. Don't pass up this opportunity! It will revolutionize your group. For information on leading your group, see the *Leader's Notes* introduction in the *Appendix*. Also, if you are leading for the first time, see *Leading for the First Time (Leadership 101)* in the *Appendix*. Also refer to the *Frequently Asked Questions (FAQs)*.

3. Share a time when you stopped growing spiritually or were drawn away from Christ for a time. What stopped your progress or drew you away? What happened to get you growing again?

 Growing

Paul described God's eternal plan and purpose for humanity in chapter 1, giving believers reason to praise him and hope in their eternal future. Paul continues in chapter 2 to give details about how God implements his plan to redeem mankind.

Read Ephesians 2.

4. In Ephesians 2:1–3, Paul describes the spiritual condition of the believers before they knew Christ as "dead in your transgressions [trespasses] and sins." What does this look like according to these verses? (See the *Study Notes* for additional insight.)

Ephesians 2:3b says, "Like the rest, we were by nature objects of wrath." What do you think this means?

5. What does it mean to be "alive with Christ" (v. 5)?

Paul reiterates that we were "dead in our transgressions" when God made us alive in Christ. Why do you think he writes this twice within the span of just a few verses?

Why is it important to constantly remember that we are saved by grace?

6. What was God's reason for raising us up with Christ according to verse 7?

How does raising us up and seating us with Christ reveal God's love and kindness?

7. In your own words, tell what role grace plays in salvation according to verses 8–10.

Why is it important that our own works don't win our salvation?

8. Although we receive our salvation through faith and not through our good works, Ephesians 2:10 calls us "God's workmanship," new people created to do good works, which God prepared for us to do. How does this mention of "good works" differ from the "works" mentioned in verse 9?

9. Paul reminded his Gentile readers that they were formerly separated from Christ and from citizenship in Israel, God's chosen people (vv. 11–13). Read verses 14–22. What does Christ's reconciliation bring to Jews and Gentiles?

10. How does Paul describe the church in verses 20–22?

   How does Paul encourage the believers to embrace unity and peace?

   How do his words motivate you to focus on unity and peace within your church and relationships?

Although we were once spiritually dead, we have been made alive in Christ and raised with him to God's right hand. Through salvation, we become part of the new creation, the restoration of all things in Christ.

Developing

Accountability means being answerable to another for our actions. Spiritual accountability happens when we invite someone into our life for the purpose of encouraging our faith journey and challenging us in specific areas of desired growth. Hebrews 3:12–13 says, "See to it, brothers, that none of you has a sinful, unbelieving heart that turns away from the living God. But encourage one another daily, as long as it is called Today, so that none of you may be hardened by sin's deceitfulness" (NIV). Opening our lives to someone and making ourselves vulnerable to their loving admonition could perhaps be one of the most difficult things to do; however, it could also result in the deepest and most lasting spiritual growth we've known.

11. Scripture tells us in Ephesians 4:25–26: "Laying aside falsehood, speak truth, each one of you with his neighbor, for we are members of one another" (NASB). With this in mind, take a moment to pair up with someone in your group to be your spiritual partner for the remainder of this study. We strongly

recommend men partner with men, and women with women. (Refer to the *Leader's Notes* for this question in the *Appendix* for information on what it means to be a spiritual partner.)

Turn to the *Personal Health Plan* in the *Appendix*. In the box that says, "WHO are you connecting with spiritually?" write your partner's name.

In the box that says, "WHAT is your next step for growth?" write one step you would like to take for growth during this study. Tell your partner what step you chose. When you check in with your partner each meeting, the "Partner's Progress" column on this chart will provide a place to record your partner's progress in the goal he or she chose.

12. Spending time together outside of group meetings helps to build stronger relationships within your group as you get to know each other better. Discuss whether your group would like to have a potluck or other type of social to celebrate together what God is doing in your group. You could plan to share a meal prior to a small group meeting or plan to follow your completion of this study with a meal together—maybe a barbecue. Appoint one or two people who can follow up with everyone outside of group time to put a plan together.

Sharing

During the past week you should have been thinking about the people in your life with whom you come into regular contact. These make up your circles of influence or *Circles of Life*.

13. Take a look at the *Circles of Life* diagram below and think of people you know in each category who need to be connected in Christian community. Write the names of two or three people in each circle.

The people who fill these circles are not there by accident. God has strategically placed each of them within your sphere of influence because he has equipped you to minister to them and share with them in ways no one else can. Consider the

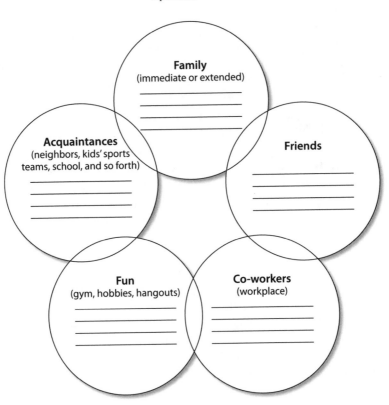

following ideas for reaching out to one or two of the people you listed and make a plan to follow through with them this week.

☐ This is a wonderful time to welcome a few friends into your group. Which of the people you listed could you invite? It's possible that you may need to help your friend overcome obstacles to coming to a place where he or she can encounter Jesus. Does your friend need a ride to the group or help with child care?

☐ Consider inviting a friend to attend a weekend church service with you and possibly plan to enjoy a meal together afterward. This can be a great opportunity to talk with someone about your faith in Jesus.

☐ Is there someone who is unable to attend your group or church but who still needs a connection? Would you be willing to have lunch or coffee with that person, catch up on life, and share something you've learned from this study? Jesus doesn't call all of us to lead small groups, but he does call every disciple to spiritually multiply his or her life over time.

Surrendering

In a world where promises are often just forgotten good intentions, it's hard to believe that anyone is faithful to keep them, but David assures us in Psalm 145:13b, "The LORD is faithful to all his promises and loving toward all he has made" (NIV). If not for the faithfulness of the Lord our God to honor his Word, we would still be living hopeless lives, destined to spend eternity separated from our awesome creator.

14. Focus on the words of David as you read Psalm 145 aloud together in an attitude of corporate worship.

15. Take a few minutes to talk about what it would take to make time with God a priority every day or even five or six days a week. Don't put time demands on yourself at first; just make it a priority to draw near to God for a few minutes each day and gradually you will desire more. Use the *Reflections* at the end of each session as a starting point.

16. Share your prayer requests as a group. Be sure to record everyone's requests on your *Prayer and Praise Report*. Use these as reminders to pray for everyone throughout the week.

    After sharing, gather in smaller circles of three or four people to pray for one another. Be careful not to pressure anyone who may not be comfortable praying aloud. When you pray for each person, you may find it meaningful to hold hands or place your hands on each other's shoulders. Jesus often touched people to communicate his care for them.

Study Notes

Dead: "Dead" is used here in a spiritual sense. It pertains to being so cut off from the God of life as to be, in effect, dead. Unbelievers, even though physically alive, are spiritually dead.

Alive: "Alive" refers to being spiritually alive, connected to the God of life. This is not possible without the power of God in our lives.

Transgressions: To transgress means to lapse or deviate from truth and uprightness. A transgression is a sin or misdeed.

Grace: Grace is God's unmerited favor. It is acceptance and goodness given toward one who cannot earn or deserve it. Finding favor in the presence of God means that God has an attitude of kindness toward us. God's grace manifests itself in the sacrificial, substitutionary death of Jesus Christ. By nature, gifts of grace cannot be earned. Grace and salvation are so connected that those who try to earn righteousness have "fallen away from grace" (Gal. 5:4).

Saved: The verb means "to save, rescue, heal." Here it denotes our being saved from penalty for sin, though in some instances the verb means to heal a person from an illness or to rescue someone from danger. Salvation takes place in the name of Jesus.

Work/works: A deed, achievement, action. In Ephesians 2:9 "works" refer to futile human attempts to save oneself. In Ephesians 2:10, they are good works that constitute the fruit of a redeemed life, the response to grace.

For Deeper Study (Optional)

God acted on behalf of humanity because he is rich in mercy. The word "rich" indicates the bountiful nature of God's mercy.

1. What does David say in Psalm 51 about what "mercy" is?

2. What does God say about himself in Jeremiah 9:24?

3. What does Jonah say about God's character in Jonah 4:2?

4. Read James 2:1–13. What does this passage say to you about mercy in the lives of believers?

Reflections

Hopefully last week you made a commitment to read, reflect, and meditate on the Word of God each day. Following are selections of Scripture provided as a starting point to drawing near to God through time with him. Read the daily verses and then record your thoughts, insights, or prayers in the space provided. On the sixth day, record a summary of what you have learned over the entire week through this study or use this space to write down how God has challenged you personally.

Day 1. "And I will be a father to you, And you shall be sons and daughters to Me," says the Lord Almighty (2 Cor. 6:18 NASB).

REFLECT

_____

_____

_____

_____

Day 2. For no one can lay any foundation other than the one we already have—Jesus Christ (1 Cor. 3:11 NLT).

REFLECT

_____

_____

_____

_____

Day 3. Nevertheless, God's solid foundation stands firm, sealed with this inscription: "The Lord knows those who are his," and, "Everyone who confesses the name of the Lord must turn away from wickedness" (2 Tim. 2:19 NIV).

REFLECT

_____

_____

_____

_____

Day 4. As the Scriptures say, "I am placing a cornerstone in Jerusalem, chosen for great honor, and anyone who trusts in him will never be disgraced." Yes, you who trust him recognize the honor God has given him. But for those who reject him, "The stone that the builders rejected has now become the cornerstone" (1 Peter 2:6–7 NLT).

REFLECT

_____

_____

_____

_____

Day 5. Simon Peter answered, "You are the Messiah, the Son of the living God." Jesus replied, "You are blessed, Simon son of John, because my Father in heaven has revealed this to you. You did not learn this from any human being. Now I say to you that you are Peter (which means "rock"), and upon this rock I will build my church, and all the powers of hell will not conquer it (Matt. 16:16–18 NLT).

REFLECT

_____

_____

_____

_____

Day 6. Use this space to record insights, thoughts, or prayers that God has given you during *Session Two* and your *Reflections* time.

SUMMARY

_____

_____

_____

_____

GOD'S MYSTERY REVEALED

Memory Verse: This mystery is that through the gospel the Gentiles are heirs together with Israel (Eph. 3:6a NIV).

British cartoonist W. E. Hill once published an adaptation of a famous perceptual illusion he titled "My Wife and My Mother-in-Law" in a 1915 publication of *Puck*, a humor magazine. In viewing this illustration, the brain tries to make sense out of the visual stimuli by assembling them into a believable image in much the same way as a jigsaw puzzle is an assemblage of fragments into a picture of ordinary things. While one person sees a young woman, another sees an old woman. And for some, another person must point out where the pieces of the visual puzzle fit together so that the brain can make sense out of them.

During the Old Testament period, God's plan for redeeming humanity remained largely a mystery. In Ephesians 3, Paul brings clarity to the mystery of redemption, pointing out how the Gentiles and Israel fit together into one new people of God.

Connecting

Begin your group discussion time by praying Psalm 86:11, which says, "Teach me your way, O LORD, and I will walk in your truth; give me an undivided heart, that I may fear your name" (NIV).

1. Most people want to live a healthy, balanced life. A regular medical checkup is a good way to measure health and spot potential problems. In the same way, a spiritual checkup is vital to your spiritual well-being. The *Personal Health Assessment* was designed to give you a quick snapshot, or pulse, of your spiritual health.

   Take a few minutes alone to complete the *Personal Health Assessment*, found in the *Appendix*. After answering each question, tally your results. Then, pair up with your spiritual partner and briefly share one purpose that is going well and one that needs a little work. Then go to the *Personal Health Plan* and record one next step you plan to take in the area of the purpose you want to work on. If you haven't established your spiritual partnership yet, do it now. (Refer to the *Session Two Leader's Notes*, for the *Developing* section for help.)

2. Have you ever discovered an insight that made other things in your life fall into perspective for you? If so, what was the insight?

Growing

The mystery now revealed to Paul and proclaimed by him was not made known clearly to previous generations of God's people (Eph. 3:5). Paul will make it known here.

Please read Ephesians 3.

3. According to 1:1 and 3:3, how did Paul receive the mystery? (See *Session One Study Notes* for insight into the "mystery.")

   Who else received God's revelation in Ephesians 3:5?

   Why does the source of Paul's information matter?

4. "This mystery is that through the gospel the Gentiles are heirs together with Israel, members together of one body, and sharers together in the promise in Christ Jesus" (3:6 NIV, emphasis added). Note the repeated word "together" in this verse. What do you think this emphasis on togetherness reveals?

5. Paul called himself the least of God's people (v. 8), yet he was given the gift of God's grace to preach to the Gentiles. Why do you think Paul considered himself the least of God's people? (See the *Study Notes* for help.)

   What was Paul called to preach (3:8–11)?

6. Believers are encouraged to approach God with freedom and in confidence. Read 3:12–13. For Paul, how does the value of the freedom spoken of in these verses compare with the value of his current circumstances? (He is in prison, not physically free.)

   What does this freedom look like in the lives of believers today?

7. Paul prays that the Ephesians will be strengthened from God's glorious riches through the power of the Holy Spirit (v. 16). What does Paul say in verse 17a about why this strength is needed? How would you put this into your own words?

8. Paul wanted the Ephesians to understand the powerful love of God so that they would learn to love one another (v. 17b). Read Ephesians 3:17–19 aloud and discuss the characteristics of God's love found in these verses.

   How does this help you comprehend the depth of love that Paul describes in verse 18?

9. Consider the powerful doxology in Ephesians 3:20–21. (See the *Study Notes* for a definition of doxology.) What might God's power in our lives look like to nonbelievers?

What must happen in a believer's life for God's power to be available to him or her?

According to these verses, what is the ultimate goal of our existence?

God's plan of redemption available through Christ was largely a mystery in the Old Testament period, especially the realization that God would bring Gentiles and Israel together as one new people of God. Paul prays for the Ephesians that they may be strengthened with power through the Holy Spirit, so that they may understand the incredible love of Christ and reveal that love to others. In this, all glory in the church and in Christ belongs to him.

Developing

God created each of us to serve him within the body of Christ. None of us can "opt out" of this service because, just as our physical body needs all of its parts to function and thrive, the spiritual body of Christ needs all of its parts as well. It is because of the vast number of needs represented by the countless people and circumstances around us that God has given every believer unique gifts. Each of us has something very special to offer to fill specific needs within the church.

10. Discuss some of the many ways that we can serve the body of Christ. Is there a particular area of service that God has put on your heart to serve either this group or your local church? If not, investigate the opportunities and pray about finding a ministry in which you can serve. As you take that first step, God will lead you to the ministry that expresses your passion.

11. On your *Personal Health Plan*, next to the "Develop" icon, answer the "WHERE are you serving?" question. If you are not currently serving, note one area where you will consider serving.

Sharing

All around us, people are struggling to find purpose for life, often looking to prestige, possessions, and people to fill the void in their life that only God can fill. In Matthew 5:14–16, Jesus said, "You are the light of the world. A city on a hill cannot be hidden. Neither do people light a lamp and put it under a bowl. Instead they put it on its stand, and it gives light to everyone in the house. In the same way, let your light shine before men, that they may see your good deeds and praise your Father in heaven" (NIV). A godly example can be a beacon of hope, shining light into a person's dark circumstances. You can become a visible reminder of God's design for others as you seek to live out his purposes in your life.

12. In the last session you were asked to write some names in the *Circles of Life* diagram. Go back to the *Circles of Life* diagram to remind yourself of the various people you come into contact with on a regular basis. Have you followed up with those you identified who need to connect with other Christians? If not, when will you contact them?

13. If you have never invited Jesus to take control of your life, why not ask him now? If you are not clear about God's gift of eternal life for everyone who believes in Jesus and how to receive this gift, take a minute to pray and ask God to help you understand what he wants you to do about trusting in Jesus.

Surrendering

Praise is focusing our hearts on God. Psalm 149:1 says, "Praise the LORD. Sing to the LORD a new song, his praise in the assembly of the saints" (NIV). It's important that we take a moment to prepare our hearts to enter into the presence of God by praising him through Scripture reading.

14. Take some time now to begin the Circle of Prayer exercise. This exercise allows for focused prayer over each person or

couple in the group. Each person or couple will have an opportunity to share any pressing needs, concerns, or struggles requiring prayer, and the rest of the group will pray for these requests. More complete instructions for this can be found in the *Leader's Notes*.

Study Notes

Least of God's People: Paul was raised as a faithful and devoted Jew, and trained by Gamaliel, one of the leading rabbis of his day. Before Paul became a Christian, he had persecuted the church, believing that Jesus was a false Messiah and that the Christians were heretics. Paul is overwhelmed that, despite this past, God had chosen him and saved him for the purpose of telling the Gentiles about Christ.

Doxology: An expression of praise to God.

Rulers and Authorities: This probably refers to both good and evil angels.

For Deeper Study (Optional)

Read the Ephesians verses indicated and see if you can identify the aspects of "mystery" contained therein.

Verse	Aspect
1:9	
3:3–4	
3:9	
5:32	
6:19	

Reflections

If you've been committed to spending time each day connecting with God through his Word, congratulations! Some experts say that it takes twenty-one repetitions to develop a new habit. By the end of this week, you'll be well on your way to cultivating new spiritual habits that will encourage you in your walk with God. This week, continue to read the daily verses, giving prayerful consideration to what you learn about God, his Spirit, and his place in your life. Then, as before, record your thoughts, insights, or prayers in the space provided. On the sixth day, record a summary of what you have learned throughout the week.

Day 1. He regarded disgrace for the sake of Christ as of greater value than the treasures of Egypt, because he was looking ahead to his reward (Heb. 11:26 NIV).

REFLECT

_____

_____

_____

_____

Day 2. Listen, my dear brothers: Has not God chosen those who are poor in the eyes of the world to be rich in faith and to inherit the kingdom he promised those who love him? (James 2:5 NIV).

REFLECT

_____

_____

_____

_____

Day 3. For whoever does the will of my Father in heaven is my brother and sister and mother (Matt. 12:50 NIV).

REFLECT

_____

_____

_____

_____

Day 4. Both the one who makes men holy and those who are made holy are of the same family. So Jesus is not ashamed to call them brothers (Heb. 2:11 NIV).

REFLECT

_____

_____

_____

_____

Day 5. And so we know and rely on the love God has for us. God is love. Whoever lives in love lives in God, and God in him (1 John 4:16 NIV).

REFLECT

_____

_____

_____

_____

Day 6. Record your weekly summary of what God has shown you in the space below.

SUMMARY

_____

_____

_____

_____

EMPOWERED TO LIVE AND SERVE

Memory Verse: You were taught, with regard to your former way of life, to put off your old self, which is being corrupted by its deceitful desires; to be made new in the attitude of your minds; and to put on the new self, created to be like God in true righteousness and holiness (Eph. 4:22–24 NIV).

Before accepting Jesus as our Lord and Savior, we often don't give much thoughtful consideration to the way we behave in our daily lives. We may be rude to someone who is inconsiderate to us. Perhaps we're prone to quarrels with loved ones. Some of us may find it second nature to talk about others with unkind words.

So what makes the difference in the life of Christ's followers? When we offer Jesus our hearts in surrender, we promise to do our best to live according to his will for our lives. Ephesians 4:22 tells us to "put off your old self, which is being corrupted by its deceitful desires." The more we read and reflect on the truth in the Bible, the more obvious it becomes that these "old-self" behaviors don't reflect our commitment to follow Christ.

It's not easy to live for Jesus and we may still revert back to some of our old tendencies from time to time, but we can be encouraged by the words of Ephesians 4:24, which says we are "created to be like God in true righteousness and holiness." We can know that God is faithful to complete us as Paul tells us in Philippians 1:6: "He who began a good work in you will carry it on to completion until the day of Christ Jesus" (NIV).

We can do our part by keeping our focus on God's desires for us and reminding ourselves daily to trust in the power of the Holy Spirit for guidance; for we know that one day we will be complete—like God in true righteousness and holiness.

Connecting

Open your group with words of praise for what God has given you through his promised Son, Jesus Christ. Thank him for what he has shown you during the last few weeks of your study of *Ephesians*, and ask him to help you become more like him in true righteousness and holiness.

1. Take five minutes to check in with your spiritual partner, or with another partner if yours is absent. Share with your partner how your time with God went this week. What is one thing you discovered? Or, what obstacles hindered you from following through? Turn to your *Personal Health Plan*. Make a note about your partner's progress and how you can pray for him or her.

2. Think back to a dramatic life change you have experienced. Maybe it was moving out of your parents' house for the first time, your wedding day, or the birth of your first child. How did you cope with the change? Was it easy or difficult for you?

Growing

Turning now from doctrinal matters to the outworking of that doctrine in practice, Paul calls the church to unity, maturity, and mutual love, because they are one body in Christ.

Read Ephesians 4.

3. Paul was in prison when he wrote to the Ephesians, and he refers to himself as a prisoner for the Lord. Paul calls the church to unity based on the things they share in common. Review the seven areas of common ground for unity found in Ephesians 4:4–6 listed below. Why is each point important for true unity in church relationships?

☐ One body   ☐ One faith

☐ One Spirit   ☐ One baptism

☐ One hope   ☐ One God and Father of

☐ One Lord   all

4. Citing Psalm 68:18, Paul refers to the gifts that God has given to believers. What are these gifts according to Ephesians 4:11?

For what purpose were these gifts given? (See Eph. 4:12–13 and the *Study Notes* for help.)

The infants in 4:14 are young Christians. What does this verse say about the tendencies of spiritually immature believers?

What can be done about those tendencies?

5. Paul exhorts believers to cast off the ungodly ways of their previous lives. Four lifestyle characteristics are identified in 4:17–19 and listed below. Read each verse and discuss why you think these characteristics are detrimental to faith.

Ephesians Reference (4:17–19)	Detriments of Characteristic (Your Notes)
in the futility of their thinking . . . verse 17	
. . . darkened in their understanding . . . verse 18a	
. . . hardening of their hearts . . . verse 18b	
. . . have given themselves over . . . to indulge in every kind of impurity . . . verse 19	

6. Believers are created to be like God in holiness and righteousness. What needs to be made new to accomplish this according to Ephesians 4:23?

7. Paul concludes the chapter with some practical tips on what the new life in Christ should look like. Read Ephesians 4:25–32. What is helpful to you in what Paul says here about:

Anger?

Talk?

8. How do the basic Christian attitudes in 4:32 contribute to unity, maturity, and mutual love?

Believers are united in Christ because of all that we share in common. We must work out the purpose of the church, in unity, through the diverse gifts that God has given to us. This means living lives of maturity as we move beyond the selfish desires that controlled us in our previous lives, and learning to relate to one another with honesty, transparency, and love, replacing anger and bitterness with kindness, compassion, and forgiveness.

Developing

First Peter 4:10–11 says, "Each one should use whatever gift he has received to serve others, faithfully administering God's grace in its various forms" (NIV). Last session we talked about using our God-given gifts to serve him in the body of Christ. Today we will spend some time exploring the gifts we are given.

9. The Bible lists the many spiritual gifts given to believers. Take five minutes and review the *Spiritual Gifts Inventory* in the *Appendix*. Discuss which of the listed gifts you believe you may have. If you are unsure, you can review the inventory with a trusted friend who knows you well. Chances are they have witnessed one or more of these gifts in your life.

Once you have an idea about what your spiritual gifts may be, discuss how you may be able to use them in ministry. Plan to investigate the opportunities available to you in your church and get involved in serving the body of Christ. It's amazing to experience God using you to fill a specific need within his church.

10. Briefly discuss the future of your group. How many of you are willing to stay together as a group and work through another study? If you have time, turn to the *Small Group Agreement* and talk about any changes you would like to make as you move forward as a group.

Sharing

Acts 4:31 says, "After they prayed, the place where they were meeting was shaken. And they were all filled with the Holy Spirit and spoke the word of God boldly" (NIV). God empowers us through his Holy Spirit to share Jesus boldly and without hindrance.

11. In *Session Two*, you identified people within your *Circles of Life* who needed a connection to Christian community. Jesus's commission in Acts 1:8 included sharing him not only within our own circles of influence (our Jerusalem), but also in Judea and Samaria and the ends of the earth. Judea included the region in which Jerusalem was located. Today, this might include neighboring communities or cities. As a group, discuss the following possible actions you can take to share Jesus with your Judea in a tangible way.

☐ Collect new blankets and/or socks for the homeless. Bring them with you next week and have someone deliver them to a ministry serving the homeless.

☐ Bring nonperishable food items to the next group meeting and designate one person to donate them to a local food bank.

☐ As a group, pick a night to volunteer to serve meals at a mission or homeless shelter.

12. On your *Personal Health Plan*, next to the "Sharing" icon, answer the "WHEN are you shepherding another person in Christ?" question.

 Surrendering

First John 3:11 says, "This is the message you heard from the beginning: We should love one another" (NIV). One way to show our love for one another is to pray focused prayer over each other's needs.

13. Last week you began praying for the specific needs of each person or couple in the group during the Circle of Prayer exercise. Take some time now to pray over those for whom the group hasn't yet prayed.

Study Notes

Gifts Given to Believers: The apostles are the foundation for Christ's church (see 2:20 and 3:6). It seems that the qualifications for being an apostle were to have seen the risen Christ, to have been sent out by him to preach the gospel, and to be working on behalf of the kingdom. Signs and wonders and miracles are also noted as marks of a true apostle in 2 Corinthians 12:12. The prophets, also laborers on the church's "foundation" (2:20), had special gifts in communicating God's messages to his people. The evangelists were traveling ministers. They went to non-Christian people and proclaimed the gospel to them. Finally, pastors and teachers are likely one gift. While the apostles, prophets, and evangelists had a universal sphere of function (the church as a whole), pastors and teachers probably served in the local churches, handling the day-to-day affairs of their congregation—administering, counseling, guiding, and discipling.

Grieving the Holy Spirit: The Holy Spirit can be saddened, or grieved, by the way we live. The Holy Spirit's power within gives new life to believers along with both the privilege of a promised future and a responsibility not to disappoint him by the way we live.

For Deeper Study (Optional)

There is one body and one Spirit—just as you were *called* to one hope when you were *called*—one Lord, one faith, one baptism; one God and Father of all, who is over all and through all and in all (Eph. 4:4–6 NIV).

Calling refers to God's sovereign call to salvation. Identify an aspect of the calling in each of the following verses:

Verse	Aspect of the Calling
Ephesians 1:18	
Romans 8:28	
Romans 11:29	
1 Corinthians 1:26	
Philippians 3:14	
2 Thessalonians 1:11	
2 Timothy 1:9	
Hebrews 3:1	
2 Peter 1:10	

Reflections

Second Timothy 3:16–17 reads, "All Scripture is God-breathed and is useful for teaching, rebuking, correcting and training in righteousness, so that the man of God may be thoroughly equipped for every good work" (NIV). Allow God's Word to train you in righteousness as you read, reflect on, and respond to the Scripture in your daily time with God this week.

Day 1. For we know that our old self was crucified with him so that the body of sin might be done away with, that we should no longer be slaves to sin (Rom. 6:6 NIV).

REFLECT

_____

_____

_____

_____

Day 2. For you have spent enough time in the past doing what pagans choose to do—living in debauchery, lust, drunkenness, orgies, carousing and detestable idolatry (1 Peter 4:3 NIV).

REFLECT

_____

_____

_____

_____

Day 3. Do not conform any longer to the pattern of this world, but be transformed by the renewing of your mind. Then you will be able to test and approve what God's will is—his good, pleasing and perfect will (Rom. 12:2 NIV).

REFLECT

_____

_____

_____

_____

Day 4. Put on the new self, which is being renewed in knowledge in the image of its Creator (Col. 3:10 NIV).

REFLECT

_____

_____

_____

_____

Day 5. Therefore, as God's chosen people, holy and dearly loved, clothe yourselves with compassion, kindness, humility, gentleness and patience (Col. 3:12 NIV).

REFLECT

_____

_____

_____

_____

Day 6. Use the following space to record your summary of how God has challenged you this week.

SUMMARY

_____

_____

_____

_____

LIVING RESPONSIBLY

Memory Verse: Be imitators of God, therefore, as dearly loved children and live a life of love, just as Christ loved us (Eph. 5:1–2b NIV).

Christ's life was one of total submission—to God the Father, to his disciples, and ultimately to all believers through his sacrifice on the cross. It was done to honor the Father through obedience to his will.

So what kind of submission does God expect from us as his cildren? Submitting to another person is an often misunderstood concept; Ephesians 5 will clarify what submission means.

 Connecting

Psalm 100:4 says, "Enter his gates with thanksgiving and his courts with praise; give thanks to him and praise his name" (NIV). As you begin your time together, offer a prayer of thanksgiving for all that God has done so far in your small group. Ask him to open your heart to receive his message for you today.

1. Check in with your spiritual partner, or with another partner if yours is absent. Talk about any challenges you are currently facing in reaching the goals you have set throughout this study. Tell your spiritual partner how he or she has helped you follow through with each step. Be sure to write down your partner's progress.

2. Briefly describe a time when you witnessed someone imitating another person. What was memorable about the circumstance?

Growing

Responsible living happens when love is the controlling focus of our relationships with others. In Ephesians 4, Paul described, in general terms, practical ways to fulfill God's purpose in the church through unity, maturity, and renewal of personal life using God's example to guide us.
Read Ephesians 5:1–6:9.

3. Just as children imitate their parents, Paul tells believers that we should imitate God. How is a believer to follow God's example according to 5:2?

4. Sin stands in stark contrast to God's holiness and love. In 5:3–5, Paul singles out sexual sins, sins of speech, and greed as worthy of special warning. Sexual sin may seem obvious, but why do you think he sees sins of speech as so serious?

Why is greed so especially serious?

5. Light and darkness cannot coexist (5:8). What does this say about the distinction between a believer's old life and new life?

6. Read Ephesians 5:6–12 aloud using the table below. Discuss how these instructions can be lived out in day-to-day life.

Verse	Instruction/Notes
Let no one deceive you with empty words, for because of such things God's wrath comes on those who are disobedient. Therefore do not be partners with them.	
For you were once darkness, but now you are light in the Lord. Live as children of light (for the fruit of the light consists in all goodness, righteousness and truth) and find out what pleases the Lord.	
Have nothing to do with the fruitless deeds of darkness, but rather expose them.	
For it is shameful even to mention what the disobedient do in secret.	

7. Living wisely includes making the most of every opportunity because the days are evil (5:15–16). What do you think Paul meant by "making the most of every opportunity"?

8. Paul tells the Ephesians to avoid getting drunk on wine, rather to be filled with the Spirit. What is the evidence of a Spirit-controlled life according to Ephesians 5:19–20?

9. Ephesians 5:21 summarizes 5:22–6:9, saying: "Submit to one another out of reverence for Christ" (NIV). How is mutual submission an expression of love?

   According to this verse, what makes this submission possible?

10. Submission in the church should follow from submission in the home. Ephesians 5:22–33 clarifies the general principle of mutual submission as it applies specifically to the relationship between husbands and wives. What should the motive and attitude of submission be?

   Describe the role of wives in submission as defined in verses 22–24. What do you think are the most significant aspects of the wife's role as defined here?

Jesus is the divine role model for husbands. According to verses 25–33, how can husbands follow Jesus's example?

11. Ephesians 6:2–3 gives a commandment with a promise. What do you think is the significance of the promise in practical terms?

How is obeying different from honoring. How are they related?

12. Paul gives a final illustration of the principle of Spirit-produced mutual submission in 6:5–9. How could applying the instructions in these verses change the climate in today's workplaces?

Loving others means avoiding sins of immorality, greed, and foolish talk, and instead living a life of goodness, righteousness, and truth, allowing the Spirit to control us. Love means mutually submitting to one another, and always keeping the best interests of the other person in mind.

Developing

During the previous four weeks, hopefully you've developed some new growth disciplines such as accountability, Scripture memorization, meditation on the Word of God, and daily time with God. Consider taking your commitment to know God better one step further this week.

13. If you've been spending time each day in personal focused prayer, doing *Reflections*, and/or meditating on God's Word, consider taking your commitment a step further this week by journaling. Read through *Journaling 101* found in the *Appendix*. Commit this week to spending a portion of your time with God journaling.

14. During *Session Two*, you should have discussed whether your group would like to have a potluck or social. Take a few minutes now to tie up any loose ends in your plan.

 Sharing

In *Session One*, we talked about Jesus's final command to his disciples in Acts 1:8: "You will be my witnesses in Jerusalem, and in all Judea and Samaria, and to the ends of the earth" (NIV). Jesus wanted his disciples to share his gospel not only with their local communities but also the world. *You* can be involved in taking the gospel to *all* nations.

15. In previous sessions you were asked identify people who need to be connected in Christian community. Return to the *Circles of Life* diagram. Outside each circle, write down one or two names of people you know who need to know Christ. Commit to praying for an opportunity to share Jesus with each of them. You may invite them to attend an outreach event with you or you may feel led to share the good news with him or her over coffee. Share your commitment with your spiritual partner. Pray together for God's Holy Spirit to give you the words to speak with boldness.

16. Prayerfully consider the following actions as a first step toward fulfilling Jesus's commission in your life.

    ☐ Hang a world map in the place where you pray at home. Pray for the world, then each continent, and then each country as the Lord leads you; or pray for the countries printed on your clothing labels as you get dressed every day.

    ☐ Send financial support to a missionary in a foreign country or a world mission organization. Your church will likely have suggestions for who this might be.

    ☐ Sponsor a child through a Christ-centered humanitarian aid organization.

Surrendering

Philippians 4:6 tells us: "Do not be anxious about anything, but in everything, by prayer and petition, with thanksgiving, present your requests to God" (NIV). Prayer represents a powerful act of surrender to the Lord as we put aside our pride and lay our burdens at his feet.

17. During the past two weeks, you've been praying for the specific needs of each person or couple in the group during the Circle of Prayer exercise. Take some time now to pray over those for whom the group hasn't yet prayed. As you did last week, allow each individual to share the specific needs or challenges they are facing. Ask for God's transforming power to bring change to their lives.

18. Turn to the *Personal Health Plan* and individually consider the "HOW are you surrendering your heart?" question. Look to the *Sample Personal Health Plan* for help. Share some of your thoughts with the group.

19. Spend a moment silently praying as David did in Psalm 139:23–24: "Search me, O God, and know my heart; test me and know my anxious thoughts. See if there is any offensive way in me, and lead me in the way everlasting" (NIV). Once you feel you've entered into an attitude of worship, sing a worship song or read Psalm 139 aloud together.

20. Share prayer requests and spend some time praying for them.

For Deeper Study (Optional)

Therefore do not be foolish, but understand what the Lord's will is (Eph. 5:17 NIV).

Look up the following verses and note what each one reveals about the will of the Lord.

Verse	The will of the Lord is:
1 Timothy 2:3–4	
Ephesians 5:18	
1 Thessalonians 4:3	
1 Peter 2:13–15	
1 Peter 2:20	
1 Thessalonians 5:18	

Reflections

The Lord promised Joshua success and prosperity in Joshua 1:8 when he said, "Do not let this Book of the Law depart from your mouth; meditate on it day and night, so that you may be careful to do everything written in it. Then you will be prosperous and successful" (NIV). We too can claim this promise for our lives as we commit to meditate on the Word of God each day. As in previous weeks, read and meditate on the daily verses and record any insights you gain in the space provided. Summarize what you have learned this week on Day 6.

Day 1. Be merciful, just as your Father is merciful (Luke 6:36 NIV). Be kind and compassionate to one another, forgiving each other, just as in Christ God forgave you (Eph. 4:32 NIV).

REFLECT

_____

_____

_____

_____

Day 2. See to it that no one takes you captive through hollow and deceptive philosophy, which depends on human tradition and the basic principles of this world rather than on Christ (Col. 2:8 NIV).

REFLECT

_____

_____

_____

_____

Day 3. "Put your trust in the light while you have it, so that you may become sons of light." When he had finished speaking, Jesus left and hid himself from them (John 12:36 NIV).

REFLECT

_____

_____

_____

_____

Day 4. Live a life of love, just as Christ loved us and gave himself up for us as a fragrant offering and sacrifice to God (Eph. 5:2 NIV).

REFLECT

_____

_____

_____

_____

Day 5. Do nothing out of selfish ambition or vain conceit, but in humility consider others better than yourselves (Phil. 2:3 NIV). Whatever you do, work at it with all your heart, as working for the Lord, not for men (Col. 3:23 NIV).

REFLECT

_____

_____

_____

_____

Day 6. Use the following space to write any thoughts God has put in your heart and mind during *Session Five* and your *Reflections* time this week.

SUMMARY

_____

_____

_____

_____

WAGING SPIRITUAL WARFARE

Memory Verse: For our struggle is not against flesh and blood, but against the rulers, against the authorities, against the powers of this dark world and against the spiritual forces of evil in the heavenly realms (Eph. 6:12 NIV).

Humankind first faced the spiritual forces of evil in the Garden of Eden when Eve was tempted by the serpent to eat the forbidden fruit of the tree of knowledge of good and evil. From the beginning, Satan, the perpetrator of evil, has done everything in his power to keep us from God—that is his ultimate goal. He does this through temptation and deception—attacking us through our weaknesses.

So how can Christians defend themselves spiritually against the evil in the world? In this session we will learn how to be strong in the Lord, putting on the armor of God, and depending wholly on him to help us wage, and win, the spiritual war we are engaged in.

 Connecting

Begin this final session with prayer. Thank God for how he has challenged and encouraged you during this study.

1. This is the last time to connect with your spiritual partner in your small group. What has God been showing you through these sessions about his faithfulness? Have you gained a more full trust in his ability to keep his promises? Check in with each other about the progress you have made in your spiritual growth during this study. Plan whether you will continue in your mentoring relationship outside your Bible study group.

2. Share with the group one thing you have learned about God and his promises during this study that has encouraged you. Also, if you have questions as a result of this study, discuss where you might find the answers.

 Growing

Paul has explained the need for unity in the body of believers. In chapter 6 he further explains that need for unity—there will be inevitable clashes with evil, and the church must be ready to fight it. Paul urges believers to be strong in the power of the Lord and to put on the "armor of God" so that they can successfully fight the spiritual battles ahead.
Read Ephesians 6.

3. When a believer becomes a child of God, he or she not only inherits God's blessings, but also becomes engaged in a struggle against the spiritual forces of wickedness. In 6:10–12, what do we learn about these forces of wickedness? What do we learn about the believer's role in this struggle?

4. This battle is being fought in the heavenly realms (Eph. 6:12). Look at the chart below. What do these verses say about who is involved in the spiritual struggle in the heavenly realms?

Ephesians Verse (NIV)	Notes
Praise be to the God and Father of our Lord Jesus Christ, who has blessed us in the heavenly realms with every spiritual blessing in Christ. 1:3	

Ephesians Verse (NIV)	Notes
. . . which he exerted in Christ when he raised him from the dead and seated him at his right hand in the heavenly realms . . . 1:20	
And God raised us up with Christ and seated us with him in the heavenly realms in Christ Jesus . . . 2:6	
His intent was that now, through the church, the manifold wisdom of God should be made known to the rulers and authorities in the heavenly realms . . . 3:10	
For our struggle is not against flesh and blood, but against the rulers, against the authorities, against the powers of this dark world and against the spiritual forces of evil in the heavenly realms. 6:12	

5. The Lord has equipped believers with everything we need for spiritual battle. The "armor of God" is not something to be put on occasionally and taken off again; it is something to be put on permanently. Using the chart below, discuss what each element of the "armor of God" represents and how believers can put on this armor in a practical sense today. See the *Study Notes* for additional insight.

God's Armor	Historic and Spiritual Meaning*
Belt of Truth—6:14	The belt cinched up the loose material on a soldier's tunic for safety. The belt that pulls together all the spiritual loose ends is "truth."
Breastplate of Righteousness—6:14	A tough breastplate covered the soldier's full torso, protecting his heart and other vital organs during battle. Righteousness, or holiness, is the Christian's protection against Satan and his schemes.
Boots of the Gospel—6:15	Roman soldiers wore boots with nails in them to grip the ground in combat. The gospel of peace is the good news that through Christ believers are at peace with God and he is on their side (Rom. 5:6–10).
Shield of Faith—6:16	The Greek word for *shield* usually refers to the large shield that protected the soldier's entire body. The believer's continual trust in God and his promises is "above all" absolutely necessary to protect Christians from temptations to every sort of sin.

God's Armor	Historic and Spiritual Meaning*
Helmet of Salvation—6:17	Satan seeks to destroy a believer's assurance of salvation with his weapons of doubt and discouragement. We must be as conscious of our confident status in Christ as if it were a helmet protecting our head.
Sword of the Spirit—6:17	God's Word is the only weapon that a believer needs; it is infinitely more powerful than any of Satan's devices.

*Adapted from *The MacArthur Bible Commentary* (Nashville: Thomas Nelson, 2005).

6. How can putting on the "armor of God" help us stand against the devil's schemes?

7. What do you think it means to pray in the Spirit (6:18)?

   How might this affect the effectiveness of our prayers?

8. Read Ephesians 6:19–20. How does Paul's prayer request in these verses help us to know how we should pray for each other?

We need to be strong in the Lord, because our struggle is a spiritual one against spiritual forces of wickedness. To wage this spiritual battle, we must put on the full "armor of God" and depend wholly on God through constant prayer.

Developing

Jesus modeled self-sacrificing service as he washed his disciples' feet in the upper room just before his arrest. He humbled himself to perform the menial task usually reserved for the lowliest of servants. In John 13:15, Jesus instructed his disciples to follow his example, saying, "I have set you an example that you should do as I have done for you" (NIV). Jesus's words should compel us to serve, but his example should inspire us to serve with hearts of humility and a willingness to get our hands dirty.

9. To serve as Jesus did, we need to be willing to humble ourselves to carry out even the most menial of tasks. This could mean

doing yard work, painting a house, or cleaning for someone who is in need. Discuss how you might serve a needy family in your church. Devise a game plan and then commit to seeing it through. You could choose one or two people who are willing to follow up with your church or a local ministry to put your plan into action.

10. If your group still needs to make decisions about continuing to meet after this session, have that discussion now. Talk about what you will study, who will lead, and where and when you will meet.

    Review your *Small Group Agreement* and evaluate how well you achieved your goals. Discuss any changes you want to make as you move forward. As your group starts a new study, this is a great time to take on a new role or change roles of service in your group. What new role will you take on? If you are uncertain, maybe your group members have some ideas for you. Remember you aren't making a lifetime commitment to the new role; it will only be for a few weeks. Maybe someone would like to share a role with you if you don't feel ready to serve solo.

Sharing

Scripture tells us that we should always be prepared to give an answer for the hope that we have found in Christ. That's what sharing Christ is all about.

11. During the course of this seven-week study, you have made many commitments to share Jesus with the people in your life, either in inviting your believing friends to grow in Christian community or by sharing the gospel in words or actions with unbelievers. Share with the group any highlights that you have experienced as you've stepped out in faith to share with others.

12. Unbelievers are not able to fully understand spiritual truth unless the Holy Spirit reveals it to them. How can this understanding change how you approach unbelievers with the gospel?

We also learned that as believers filled with the Holy Spirit, we are given power to share the message of Christ boldly. How might this alleviate our fears about sharing the truth about Jesus with others? What will you do as a result of this new insight? See question 13 for an exercise to get you started.

13. Telling your own story is a powerful way to share Jesus with others. Turn to *Telling Your Story* in the *Appendix*. Review this with your spiritual partner. Begin developing your story by taking a few minutes to share briefly what your life was like before you knew Christ. (If you haven't yet committed your life to Christ or are not sure, you can find information about this in the *Sharing* section of *Session Three*. If you became a Christian at a very young age and don't remember what life was like before Christ, reflect on what you have seen in the life of someone close to you.) Make notes about this aspect of your story below and commit to writing it out this week. Then, spend some time individually developing your complete story using the *Telling Your Story* exercise in the *Appendix*.

_____

_____

_____

 Surrendering

Scripture tells us in Proverbs 15:29: "The LORD . . . hears the prayer of the righteous" (NIV).

14. Look back over the *Prayer and Praise Report*. Are there any answered prayers? Spend a few minutes sharing these in simple,

one-sentence prayers of thanks to God. It's important to share your praises along with prayer requests each week so you can see where God is working in your lives.

Share any new prayer requests you have with the group and record them on the *Prayer and Praise Report*.

15. Close by sharing and praying for your prayer requests and take a couple of minutes to review the praises you have recorded over the past few weeks on the *Prayer and Praise Report*. Thank God for what he's done in your group during this study.

Study Notes

Satan, Devil: A literal, evil being viciously opposed to God and to his children (Rev. 12:17). Various attributes of the devil are brought to the surface in the New Testament: He is a tempter (Matt. 4:1ff), liar, murderer (John 8:44), betrayer (John 13:2), perpetual sinner (1 John 3:8), full of hate (1 Peter 5:8), and conceited (1 Tim. 3:6). The works of the devil are always painful and many times subtle. He longs to bring suffering on believers. He is a devious schemer. Adapted from *Mounce's Complete Expository Dictionary* (Grand Rapids: Zondervan, 2006).

For Deeper Study (Optional)

Ephesians is a wealth of information about how we are to walk with God. Read the verses indicated below and see if you can identify the "walking orders" contained in each one.

Verse	Walking Order
2:2	
2:10	
4:1	
4:17	
5:2	
5:8	
5:15	

Reflections

Get into harmony with God as you spend time with him this week. Read and reflect on the daily verses. Then record your thoughts, insights, or prayers in the *Reflect* sections that follow. On the sixth day record your summary of what God has taught you this week.

Day 1. Be self-controlled and alert. Your enemy the devil prowls around like a roaring lion looking for someone to devour. Resist him, standing firm in the faith, because you know that your brothers throughout the world are undergoing the same kind of sufferings (1 Peter 5:8–9 NIV).

REFLECT

_____

_____

_____

_____

Day 2. Submit yourselves, then, to God. Resist the devil, and he will flee from you (James 4:7 NIV).

REFLECT

_____

_____

_____

_____

Day 3. Therefore, prepare your minds for action; be self-controlled; set your hope fully on the grace to be given you when Jesus Christ is revealed (1 Peter 1:13 NIV).

REFLECT

_____

_____

_____

_____

Day 4. But since we belong to the day, let us be self-controlled, putting on faith and love as a breastplate, and the hope of salvation as a helmet (1 Thess. 5:8 NIV).

REFLECT

_____

_____

_____

_____

Day 5. Do not be anxious about anything, but in everything, by prayer and petition, with thanksgiving, present your requests to God (Phil. 4:6 NIV).

REFLECT

_____

_____

_____

_____

Day 6. Record your summary of what God has taught you this week.

SUMMARY

_____

_____

_____

_____

FREQUENTLY ASKED QUESTIONS

What do we do on the first night of our group?

Like all fun things in life—have a party! A "get to know you" coffee, dinner, or dessert is a great way to launch a new study. You may want to review the *Small Group Agreement* and share the names of a few friends you can invite to join you. But most importantly, have fun before your study time begins.

Where do we find new members for our group?

This can be challenging, especially for new groups that have only a few people or for existing groups that lose a few people along the way. We encourage you to pray with your group and then brainstorm a list of people from work, church, your neighborhood, your children's school, family, the gym, and so forth. Then have each group member invite several of the people on his or her list. Another good strategy is to ask church leaders to make an announcement that your group is open to new members.

No matter how you find members, it's vital that you stay on the lookout for new people to join your group. All groups tend to go through healthy attrition—the result of moves, releasing new leaders, ministry opportunities, and so forth—and if the group gets too small, it could be at risk of shutting down. If you and your group stay open, you'll be amazed at the people God sends your way. The next person just might become a friend for life. You never know!

How long will this group meet?

It's totally up to the group—once you come to the end of this study. Most groups meet weekly for at least their first six months together, but every other week can work as well. We strongly recommend that the group meet for the first six months on a weekly basis if at all possible. This allows for continuity, and if people miss a meeting they aren't gone for a whole month.

At the end of this study, each group member may decide whether he or she wants to continue on for another study. Some groups launch relationships that last for years, and others are stepping-stones into another group experience. Either way, enjoy the journey.

What if this group is not working for me?

Personality conflicts, life stage differences, geographical distance, level of spiritual maturity, or any number of things can cause you to feel the group doesn't work for you. Relax. Pray for God's direction, and at the end of this study decide whether to continue with this group or find another. You don't buy the first car you look at or marry the first person you date, and the same goes with a group. Don't bail out before the study is finished—God might have something to teach you. Also, don't run from conflict or prejudge people before you have given them a chance. God is still working in you too!

Who is the leader?

Most groups have an official leader. But ideally, the group will mature and members will share the facilitation of meetings. We have discovered that healthy groups share hosting and leading of the group. This model ensures that all members grow, give their unique contribution, and develop their gifts. This study guide and the Holy Spirit can keep things on track even when you share leadership. Christ has promised to be in your midst as you gather. Ultimately, God is your leader each step of the way.

How do we handle the child care needs in our group?

This can be a sensitive issue. We suggest that you empower the group to openly brainstorm solutions. You may try one option that works for a while and then adjust over time. Our favorite approach is for adults to meet in the living room or dining room, and share the cost of a babysitter (or two) who can be with the kids in a different part of the house. In this way, parents don't have to be away from their children all evening when their children are too young to be left at home. A second option is to use one home for the kids and a second home (close by) for the adults. A third idea is to rotate the responsibility of providing a lesson or care for the children either in the same home or in another home nearby. This can be an incredible blessing for kids. Finally, the most common idea is to decide that you need to have a night to invest in your spiritual lives individually or as a couple, and make your own arrangements for child care. No matter what decision the group makes, the best approach is to dialogue openly about both the problem and the solution.

SMALL GROUP AGREEMENT

Our Purpose

To transform our spiritual lives by cultivating our spiritual health in a healthy small group community. In addition, we:

_____

_____

_____

Our Values

Group Attendance	To give priority to the group meeting. We will call or e-mail if we will be late or absent. (Completing the *Small Group Calendar* will minimize this issue.)
Safe Environment	To help create a safe place where people can be heard and feel loved. (Please, no quick answers, snap judgments, or simple fixes.)
Respect Differences	To be gentle and gracious to people with different spiritual maturity, personal opinions, temperaments, or imperfections. We are all works in progress.
Confidentiality	To keep anything that is shared strictly confidential and within the group, and avoid sharing improper information about those outside the group.
Encouragement for Growth	To be not just takers but givers of life. We want to spiritually multiply our lives by serving others with our God-given gifts.

Welcome for Newcomers	To keep an open chair and share Jesus's dream of finding a shepherd for every sheep.
Shared Ownership	To remember that every member is a minister and to ensure that each attender will share a small team role or responsibility over time. (See the *Team Roles*.)
Rotating Hosts/ Leaders and Homes	To encourage different people to host the group in their homes, and to rotate the responsibility of facilitating each meeting. (See the *Small Group Calendar*.)

Our Expectations

- Refreshments/mealtimes _____
- Child care _____
- When we will meet (day of week) _____
- Where we will meet (place) _____
- We will begin at (time) _____ and end at _____
- We will do our best to have some or all of us attend a worship service together. Our primary worship service time will be _____
- Date of this agreement _____
- Date we will review this agreement again _____
- Who (other than the leader) will review this agreement at the end of this study _____

TEAM ROLES

The Bible makes clear that every member, not just the small group leader, is a minister in the body of Christ. In a healthy small group, every member takes on some small role or responsibility. It can be more fun and effective if you team up on these roles.

Review the team roles and responsibilities below, and have each member volunteer for a role or participate on a team. If someone doesn't know where to serve or is holding back, as a group, suggest a team or role. It's best to have one or two people on each team so you have each of the five purposes covered. Serving in even a small capacity will not only help your leader but also will make the group more fun for everyone. Don't hold back. Join a team!

The opportunities below are broken down by the five purposes and then by a *crawl* (beginning), *walk* (intermediate), or *run* (advanced) role. Try to cover at least the crawl and walk roles, and select a role that matches your group, your gifts, and your maturity.

Team Roles	Team Player(s)

CONNECTING TEAM (Fellowship and Community Building)

Crawl: Host a social event or group activity in the first week or two. _____

Walk: Create a list of uncommitted friends and then invite them to an open house or group social. _____

Run: Plan a twenty-four-hour retreat or weekend getaway for the group. Lead the *Connecting* time each week for the group. _____

GROWING TEAM (Discipleship and Spiritual Growth)

Crawl: Coordinate the spiritual partners for the group. Facilitate a three- or four-person discussion circle during the Bible study portion of your meeting. Coordinate the discussion circles. _____

Walk: Tabulate the *Personal Health Plans* in a summary to let people know how you're doing as a group. Encourage personal devotions through group discussions and pairing up with spiritual (accountability) partners. _____

Run: Take the group on a prayer walk, or plan a day of solitude, fasting, or personal retreat. _____

SERVING TEAM (Discovering Your God-Given Design for Ministry)

Crawl: Ensure that every member finds a group role or team he or she enjoys. _____

Walk: Have every member take a gift test and determine your group's gifts. Plan a ministry project together. _____

Run: Help each member decide on a way to use his or her unique gifts somewhere in the church. _____

SHARING TEAM (Sharing and Evangelism)

Crawl: Coordinate the group's *Prayer and Praise Report* of friends and family who don't know Christ. _____

Walk: Search for group mission opportunities and plan a cross-cultural group activity. _____

Run: Take a small group "vacation" to host a six-week group in your neighborhood or office. Then come back together with your current group. _____

SURRENDERING TEAM (Surrendering Your Heart to Worship)

Crawl: Maintain the group's *Prayer and Praise Report* or journal. _____

Walk: Lead a brief time of worship each week (at the beginning or end of your meeting). _____

Run: Plan a more unique time of worship. _____

SMALL GROUP CALENDAR

Planning and calendaring can help ensure the greatest participation at every meeting. At the end of each meeting, review this calendar. Be sure to include a regular rotation of host homes and leaders, and don't forget birthdays, socials, church events, holidays, and mission/ministry projects.

Date	Lesson	Dessert/Meal	Role

PERSONAL HEALTH ASSESSMENT

	Just Beginning	Getting Going	Well Developed

CONNECTING with God's Family

I am deepening my understanding of and friendship with God in community with others.	1 2 3 4 5
I am growing in my ability both to share and to show my love to others.	1 2 3 4 5
I am willing to share my real needs for prayer and support from others.	1 2 3 4 5
I am resolving conflict constructively and am willing to forgive others.	1 2 3 4 5
CONNECTING Total	_____

GROWING to Be Like Christ

I have a growing relationship with God through regular time in the Bible and in prayer (spiritual habits).	1 2 3 4 5
I am experiencing more of the characteristics of Jesus Christ (love, patience, gentleness, courage, self-control, etc.) in my life.	1 2 3 4 5
I am avoiding addictive behaviors (food, television, busyness, and the like) to meet my needs.	1 2 3 4 5
I am spending time with a Christian friend (spiritual partner) who celebrates and challenges my spiritual growth.	1 2 3 4 5
GROWING Total	_____

79

	Just Beginning	Getting Going	Well Developed

DEVELOPING Your Gifts to Serve Others

I have discovered and am further developing my unique God-given design.   1 2 3 4 5

I am regularly praying for God to show me opportunities to serve him and others.   1 2 3 4 5

I am serving in a regular (once a month or more) ministry in the church or community.   1 2 3 4 5

I am a team player in my small group by sharing some group role or responsibility.   1 2 3 4 5

DEVELOPING Total   _____

SHARING Your Life Mission Every Day

I am cultivating relationships with non-Christians and praying for God to give me natural opportunities to share his love.   1 2 3 4 5

I am praying and learning about where God can use me and our group cross-culturally for missions.   1 2 3 4 5

I am investing my time in another person or group who needs to know Christ.   1 2 3 4 5

I am regularly inviting unchurched or unconnected friends to my church or small group.   1 2 3 4 5

SHARING Total   _____

SURRENDERING Your Life for God's Pleasure

I am experiencing more of the presence and power of God in my everyday life.   1 2 3 4 5

I am faithfully attending services and my small group to worship God.   1 2 3 4 5

I am seeking to please God by surrendering every area of my life (health, decisions, finances, relationships, future, etc.) to him.   1 2 3 4 5

I am accepting the things I cannot change and becoming increasingly grateful for the life I've been given.   1 2 3 4 5

SURRENDERING Total   _____

Personal Health Assessment

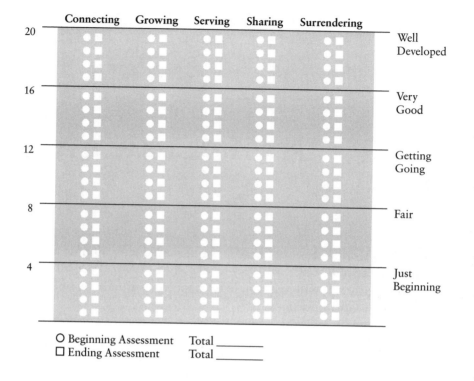

O Beginning Assessment   Total _____
□ Ending Assessment   Total _____

PERSONAL HEALTH PLAN

This worksheet could become your single most important feature in this study. On it you can record your personal priorities before the Father. It will help you live a healthy spiritual life, balancing all five of God's purposes.

PURPOSE	PLAN
CONNECT	WHO are you connecting with spiritually?
GROW	WHAT is your next step for growth?
DEVELOP	WHERE are you serving?
SHARE	WHEN are you shepherding another in Christ?
SURRENDER	HOW are you surrendering your heart to God?

DATE	MY PROGRESS	PARTNER'S PROGRESS

Personal Health Plan

DATE	MY PROGRESS	PARTNER'S PROGRESS

SAMPLE PERSONAL HEALTH PLAN

This worksheet could become your single most important feature in this study. On it you can record your personal priorities before the Father. It will help you live a healthy spiritual life, balancing all five of God's purposes.

PURPOSE	PLAN
CONNECT	WHO are you connecting with spiritually?
	Bill and I will meet weekly by e-mail or phone
GROW	WHAT is your next step for growth?
	Regular devotions or journaling my prayers 2×/week
DEVELOP	WHERE are you serving?
	Serving in children's ministry Go through GIFTS Assessment
SHARE	WHEN are you shepherding another in Christ?
	Shepherding Bill at lunch or hosting a starter group in the fall
SURRENDER	HOW are you surrendering your heart?
	Help with our teenager New job situation

DATE	MY PROGRESS	PARTNER'S PROGRESS
3/5	Talked during our group	Figured out our goals together
3/12	Missed our time together	Missed our time together
3/26	Met for coffee and review of my goals	Met for coffee
4/10	E-mailed prayer requests	Bill sent me his prayer requests
5/5	Great start on personal journaling	Read Mark 1–6 in one sitting!
5/12	Traveled and not doing well this week	Journaled about Christ as healer
5/26	Back on track	Busy and distracted; asked for prayer
6/1	Need to call Children's Pastor	
6/26	Group did a serving project together	Agreed to lead group worship
6/30	Regularly rotating leadership	Led group worship–great job!
7/5	Called Jim to see if he's open to joining our group	Wanted to invite somebody, but didn't
7/12	Preparing to start a group in fall	
7/30	Group prayed for me	Told friend something I'm learning about Christ
8/5	Overwhelmed but encouraged	Scared to lead worship
8/15	Felt heard and more settled	Issue with wife
8/30	Read book on teens	Glad he took on his fear

SPIRITUAL GIFTS INVENTORY

A spiritual gift is given to each of us as a means of helping the entire church.

1 Corinthians 12:7 (NLT)

A spiritual gift is a special ability, given by the Holy Spirit to every believer at their conversion. Although spiritual gifts are given when the Holy Spirit enters new believers, their use and purpose need to be understood and developed as we grow spiritually. A spiritual gift is much like a muscle; the more you use it, the stronger it becomes.

A Few Truths about Spiritual Gifts

1. Only believers have spiritual gifts. 1 Corinthians 2:14
2. You can't earn or work for a spiritual gift. Ephesians 4:7
3. The Holy Spirit decides what gifts I get. 1 Corinthians 12:11
4. I am to develop the gifts God gives me. Romans 11:29; 2 Timothy 1:6
5. It's a sin to waste the gifts God gave me. 1 Corinthians 4:1–2; Matthew 25:14–30
6. Using my gifts honors God and expands me. John 15:8

Gifts Inventory

God wants us to know what spiritual gift(s) he has given us. One person can have many gifts. The goal is to find the areas in which the Holy Spirit seems to have supernaturally empowered our service to others. These gifts are to be used to minister to others and build up the body of Christ.

There are four main lists of gifts found in the Bible in Romans 12:3–8; 1 Corinthians 12:1–11, 27–31; Ephesians 4:11–12; and 1 Peter 4:9–11. There are other passages that mention or illustrate gifts not included in these lists. As you read through this list, prayerfully consider whether the biblical definition describes you. Remember, you can have more than one gift, but everyone has at least one.

ADMINISTRATION (Organization)—1 Corinthians 12

This is the ability to recognize the gifts of others and recruit them to a ministry. It is the ability to organize and manage people, resources, and time for effective ministry.

APOSTLE—1 Corinthians 12

This is the ability to start new churches/ventures and oversee their development.

DISCERNMENT—1 Corinthians 12

This is the ability to distinguish between the spirit of truth and the spirit of error; to detect inconsistencies in another's life and confront in love.

ENCOURAGEMENT (Exhortation)—Romans 12

This is the ability to motivate God's people to apply and act on biblical principles, especially when they are discouraged or wavering in their faith. It is also the ability to bring out the best in others and challenge them to develop their potential.

EVANGELISM—Ephesians 4

This is the ability to communicate the gospel of Jesus Christ to unbelievers in a positive, nonthreatening way and to sense opportunities to share Christ and lead people to respond with faith.

FAITH—1 Corinthians 12

This is the ability to trust God for what cannot be seen and to act on God's promise, regardless of what the circumstances indicate. This includes a willingness to risk failure in pursuit of a God-given vision, expecting God to handle the obstacles.

GIVING—Romans 12

This is the ability to generously contribute material resources and/or money beyond the 10 percent tithe so that the church may grow and be strengthened. It includes the ability to manage money so it may be given to support the ministry of others.

HOSPITALITY—1 Peter 4:9–10

This is the ability to make others, especially strangers, feel warmly welcomed, accepted, and comfortable in the church family and the ability to coordinate factors that promote fellowship.

LEADERSHIP—Romans 12

This is the ability to clarify and communicate the purpose and direction ("vision") of a ministry in a way that attracts others to get involved, including the ability to motivate others, by example, to work together in accomplishing a ministry goal.

MERCY—Romans 12

This is the ability to manifest practical, compassionate, cheerful love toward suffering members of the body of Christ.

PASTORING (Shepherding)—Ephesians 4

This is the ability to care for the spiritual needs of a group of believers and equip them for ministry. It is also the ability to nurture a small group in spiritual growth and assume responsibility for their welfare.

PREACHING—Romans 12

This is the ability to publicly communicate God's Word in an inspired way that convinces unbelievers and both challenges and comforts believers.

SERVICE—Romans 12

This is the ability to recognize unmet needs in the church family, and take the initiative to provide practical assistance quickly, cheerfully, and without a need for recognition.

TEACHING—Ephesians 4

This is the ability to educate God's people by clearly explaining and applying the Bible in a way that causes them to learn; it is the ability to equip and train other believers for ministry.

WISDOM—1 Corinthians 12

This is the ability to understand God's perspective on life situations and share those insights in a simple, understandable way.

TELLING YOUR STORY

First, don't underestimate the power of your testimony. Revelation 12:11 says, "They have defeated [Satan] by the blood of the Lamb and by their testimony. And they did not love their lives so much that they were afraid to die" (NLT).

A simple three-point approach is very effective in communicating your personal testimony. The approach focuses on before you trusted Christ, how you surrendered to him, and the difference in you since you've been walking with him. If you became a Christian at a very young age and don't remember what life was like before Christ, reflect on what you have seen in the lives of others. Before you begin, pray and ask God to give you the right words.

Before You Knew Christ

Simply tell what your life was like before you surrendered to Christ. What was the key problem, emotion, situation, or attitude you were dealing with? What motivated you? What were your actions? How did you try to satisfy your inner needs? Create an interesting picture of your preconversion life and problems, and then explain what created a need and interest in Christian things.

How You Came to Know Christ

How were you converted? Simply tell the events and circumstances that caused you to consider Christ as the solution to your needs. Take time to identify the steps that brought you to the point of trusting Christ. Where were you? What was happening at the time? What people or problems influenced your decision?

The Difference Christ Has Made in Your Life

What is different about your life in Christ? How has his forgiveness impacted you? How have your thoughts, attitudes, and emotions changed? What problems have been resolved or changed? Share how Christ is meeting your needs and what a relationship with him means to you now. This should be the largest part of your story.

Tips

- Don't use jargon: don't sound churchy, preachy, or pious.
- Stick to the point. Your conversion and new life in Christ should be the main points.
- Be specific. Include events, genuine feelings, and personal insights, both before and after conversion, which people would be interested in and that clarify your main point. This makes your testimony easier to relate to. Assume you are sharing with someone with no knowledge of the Christian faith.
- Be current. Tell what is happening in your life with God now, today.
- Be honest. Don't exaggerate or portray yourself as living a perfect life with no problems. This is not realistic. The simple truth of what God has done in your life is all the Holy Spirit needs to convict someone of their sin and convince them of his love and grace.
- Remember, it's the Holy Spirit who convicts. You need only be obedient and tell your story.
- When people reply to your efforts to share with statements like "I don't believe in God," "I don't believe the Bible is God's Word," or "How can a loving God allow suffering?" how can we respond to these replies?

- Above all, keep a positive attitude. Don't be defensive.
- Be sincere. This will speak volumes about your confidence in your faith.
- Don't be offended. It's not you they are rejecting.
- Pray—silently on-the-spot. Don't proceed without asking for God's help about the specific question. Seek his guidance on how, or if, you should proceed at this time.
- In God's wisdom, choose to do one of the following:
  - Postpone sharing at this time.
  - Answer their objections, if you can.
  - Promise to research their questions and return answers later.

Step 1. Everywhere Jesus went he used stories, or parables, to demonstrate our need for salvation. Through these stories, he helped people see the error of their ways, leading them to turn to him. Your story can be just as powerful today. Begin to develop your story by sharing what your life was like before you knew Christ. (If you haven't yet committed your life to Christ, or became a Christian at a very young age and don't remember what life was like before Christ, reflect on what you have seen in the life of someone close to you.) Make notes about this aspect of your story below and commit to writing it out this week.

_____

_____

_____

Step 2. Sit in groups of two or three people for this discussion. Review the "How You Came to Know Christ" section. Begin to develop this part of your story by sharing within your circle. Make notes about this aspect of your story below and commit to writing it out this week.

_____

_____

_____

Step 2b. Connecting: Go around the group and share about a time you were stopped cold while sharing Christ, by a question you couldn't answer. What happened?

Step 2c. Sharing: Previously we talked about the questions and objections we receive that stop us from continuing to share our faith with someone. These questions/objections might include:

- "I don't believe in God."
- "I don't believe the Bible is God's Word."
- "How can a loving God allow suffering?"

How can we respond to these replies?

Step 3. Subgroup into groups of two or three people for this discussion. Review "The Difference Christ Has Made in Your Life" section. Share the highlights of this part of your story within your circle. Make notes about this aspect of your story below and commit to writing it out this week.

_____

_____

_____

Step 3b. Story: There's nothing more exciting than a brand-new believer. My wife became a Christian four years before I met her. She was a flight attendant at the time. Her zeal to introduce others to Jesus was reminiscent of the woman at the well who ran and got the whole town out to see Jesus.

My wife immediately began an international organization of Christian flight attendants for fellowship and for reaching out to others in their profession. She organized events where many people came to Christ, and bid for trips with another flight attendant who was a Christian so they could witness on the planes. They even bid for the shorter trips so they could talk to as many different people as possible. They had a goal for every flight to talk to at least one person about Christ, and to be encouraged by at least one person who already knew him. God met that request every time.

In her zeal, however, she went home to her family over the holidays and vacations and had little or no success. Later she would realize that she pressed them too hard. Jesus said a prophet is without honor in his own town, and I think the same goes for family. That's because members of your family think they know you, and are more likely to ignore changes, choosing instead to see you as they've always seen you. "Isn't this the carpenter's son—the son of Joseph?" they said of Jesus. "Don't we know this guy?"

With family members you have to walk with Christ openly and be patient. Change takes time. And remember, we don't save anyone. We just introduce them to Jesus through telling our own story. God does the rest.

Step 4. As a group, review *Telling Your Story*. Share which part of your story is the most difficult for you to tell. Which is the easiest for you? If you have time, a few of you share your story with the group.

Step 5. Throughout this study we have had the opportunity to develop our individual testimonies. One way your group can serve each other is to provide a safe forum for "practicing" telling your stories. Continue to take turns sharing your testimonies now. Set a time limit—say two to three minutes each. Don't miss this great opportunity to get to know one another better and encourage each other's growth too.

SERVING COMMUNION

Churches vary in their treatment of communion (or the Lord's Supper). We offer one simple form by which a small group can share this experience together. You can adapt this as necessary, or omit it from your group altogether, depending on your church's beliefs.

Steps in Serving Communion

1. Open by sharing about God's love, forgiveness, grace, mercy, commitment, tenderheartedness, faithfulness, etc., out of your personal journey (connect with the stories of those in the room).
2. Read one or several of the passages listed below.
3. Pray and pass the bread around the circle.
4. When everyone has been served, remind them that this represents Jesus's broken body on their behalf. Simply state, "Jesus said, 'Do this in remembrance of me' (Luke 22:19 NIV). Let us eat together," and eat the bread as a group.
5. Then read the rest of the passage: "In the same way, after the supper he took the cup, saying, 'This cup is the new covenant in my blood, which is poured out for you'" (Luke 22:20 NIV).
6. Pray, and serve the cups, either by passing a small tray, serving them individually, or having members pick up a cup from the table.
7. When everyone has been served, remind them the juice represents Christ's blood shed for them, then simply state, "Take and drink in remembrance of him. Let us drink together."
8. Finish by singing a simple song, listening to a praise song, or having a time of prayer in thanks to God.

Communion passages: Matthew 26:26–29; Mark 14:22–25; Luke 22:14–20; 1 Corinthians 10:16–21; 11:17–34.

PERFORMING A FOOTWASHING

Scripture: John 13:1–17. Jesus makes it quite clear to his disciples that his position as the Father's Son includes being a servant rather than power and glory only. To properly understand the scene and the intention of Jesus, we must realize that the washing of feet was the duty of slaves and indeed of non-Jewish rather than Jewish slaves. Jesus placed himself in the position of a servant. He displayed to the disciples self-sacrifice and love. In view of his majesty, only the symbolic position of a slave was adequate to open their eyes and keep them from lofty illusions. The point of footwashing, then, is to correct the attitude that Jesus discerned in the disciples. It constitutes the permanent basis for mutual service, service in your group and for the community around you, which is the responsibility of all Christians.

When to Implement

There are three primary places we would recommend you insert a footwashing: during a break in the Surrendering section of your group; during a break in the Growing section of your group; or at the closing of your group. A special time of prayer for each person as he or she gets his or her feet washed can be added to the footwashing time.

SURRENDERING AT THE CROSS

Surrendering everything to God is one of the most challenging aspects of following Jesus. It involves a relationship built on trust and faith. Each of us is in a different place on our spiritual journey. Some of us have known the Lord for many years, some are new in our faith, and some may still be checking God out. Regardless, we all have things that we still want control over—things we don't want to give to God because we don't know what he will do with them. These things are truly more important to us than God is—they have become our god.

We need to understand that God wants us to be completely devoted to him. If we truly love God with all our heart, soul, strength, and mind (Luke 10:27), we will be willing to give him everything.

Steps in Surrendering at the Cross

1. You will need some small pieces of paper and pens or pencils for people to write down the things they want to sacrifice/surrender to God.
2. If you have a wooden cross, hammers, and nails you can have the members nail their sacrifices to the cross. If you don't have a wooden cross, get creative. Think of another way to symbolically relinquish the sacrifices to God. You might use a fireplace to burn them in the fire as an offering to the Lord. The point is giving to the Lord whatever hinders your relationship with him.

3. Create an atmosphere conducive to quiet reflection and prayer. Whatever this quiet atmosphere looks like for your group, do the best you can to create a peaceful time to meet with God.

4. Once you are settled, prayerfully think about the points below. Let the words and thoughts draw you into a heart-to-heart connection with your Lord Jesus Christ.

☐ *Worship him.* Ask God to change your viewpoint so you can worship him through a surrendered spirit.

☐ *Humble yourself.* Surrender doesn't happen without humility. James 4:6–7 says: "'God opposes the proud but gives grace to the humble.' Submit yourselves, then, to God" (NIV).

☐ *Surrender your mind, will, and emotions.* This is often the toughest part of surrendering. What do you sense God urging you to give him so you can have the kind of intimacy he desires with you? Our hearts yearn for this kind of connection with him; let go of the things that stand between you.

☐ *Write out your prayer.* Write out your prayer of sacrifice and surrender to the Lord. This may be an attitude, a fear, a person, a job, a possession—anything that God reveals is a hindrance to your relationship with him.

5. After writing out your sacrifice, take it to the cross and offer it to the Lord. Nail your sacrifice to the cross, or burn it as a sacrifice in the fire.

6. Close by singing, praying together, or taking communion. Make this time as short or as long as seems appropriate for your group.

Surrendering to God is life-changing and liberating. God desires that we be overcomers! First John 4:4 says, "You, dear children, are from God and have overcome . . . because the one who is in you is greater than the one who is in the world" (NIV).

JOURNALING 101

Henri Nouwen says effective and lasting ministry *for* God grows out of a quiet place alone *with* God. This is why journaling is so important.

The greatest adventure of our lives is found in the daily pursuit of knowing, growing in, serving, sharing, and worshiping Christ forever. This is the essence of a purposeful life: to see all these biblical purposes fully formed and balanced in our lives. Only then are we "complete in Christ" (Col. 1:28 NASB).

David poured his heart out to God by writing psalms. The book of Psalms contains many of his honest conversations with God in written form, including expressions of every imaginable emotion on every aspect of his life. Like David, we encourage you to select a strategy to integrate God's Word and journaling into your devotional time. Use any of the following resources:

- Bible
- Bible reading plan
- Devotional
- Topical Bible study plan

Before and after you read a portion of God's Word, speak to God in honest reflection in the form of a written prayer. You may begin this time by simply finishing the sentence "Father, . . . ," "Yesterday, Lord, . . . ," or "Thank you, God, for, ..." Share with him where you are at the present moment; express your hurts, disappointments, frustrations, blessings, victories, and gratefulness. Whatever you do with your journal, make a plan that fits you, so you'll have a positive experience. Consider sharing highlights of your progress and experiences with some or all of your group members, especially your spiritual partner. You may find they want to join and even encourage you in this journey. Most of all, enjoy the ride and cultivate a more authentic, growing walk with God.

PRAYER AND PRAISE REPORT

Briefly share your prayer requests with the large group, making notations below. Then gather in small groups of two to four to pray for each other.

Date: _____

Prayer Requests

_____

_____

_____

_____

_____

Praise Reports

_____

_____

_____

_____

_____

Prayer and Praise Report

Briefly share your prayer requests with the large group, making notations below. Then gather in small groups of two to four to pray for each other.

Date: _____

Prayer Requests

_____

_____

_____

_____

_____

Praise Reports

_____

_____

_____

_____

_____

Prayer and Praise Report

Briefly share your prayer requests with the large group, making notations below. Then gather in small groups of two to four to pray for each other.

Date: _____

Prayer Requests

_____

_____

_____

_____

_____

Praise Reports

_____

_____

_____

_____

_____

Prayer and Praise Report

Briefly share your prayer requests with the large group, making notations below. Then gather in small groups of two to four to pray for each other.

Date: _____

Prayer Requests

_____

_____

_____

_____

_____

Praise Reports

_____

_____

_____

_____

_____

Prayer and Praise Report

Briefly share your prayer requests with the large group, making notations below. Then gather in small groups of two to four to pray for each other.

Date: _____

Prayer Requests

_____

_____

_____

_____

_____

Praise Reports

_____

_____

_____

_____

_____

SMALL GROUP ROSTER

Name	Address	Phone	E-mail Address	Team or Role	When/How to Contact You
Bill Jones	7 Alvalar Street L.F. 92665	766-2255	bjones@aol.com	Socials	Evenings After 5

(Pass your book around your group at your first meeting to get everyone's name and contact information.)

Name	Address	Phone	E-mail Address	Team or Role	When/How to Contact You

LEADING FOR THE FIRST TIME
LEADERSHIP 101

Sweaty palms are a healthy sign. The Bible says God is gracious to the humble. Remember who is in control; the time to worry is when you're not worried. Those who are soft in heart (and sweaty-palmed) are those whom God is sure to speak through.

Seek support. Ask your leader, coleader, or close friend to pray for you and prepare with you before the session. Walking through the study will help you anticipate potentially difficult questions and discussion topics.

Bring your uniqueness to the study. Lean into who you are and how God wants you to uniquely lead the study.

Prepare. Prepare. Prepare. Go through the session several times. If you are using the DVD, listen to the teaching segment and *Leader Lifter*. Consider writing in a journal or fasting for a day to prepare yourself for what God wants to do.

Don't wait until the last minute to prepare.

Ask for feedback so you can grow. Perhaps in an e-mail or on cards handed out at the study, have everyone write down three things you did well and one thing you could improve on. Don't get defensive, but show an openness to learn and grow.

Prayerfully consider launching a new group. This doesn't need to happen overnight, but God's heart is for this to happen over time. Not all Christians are called to be leaders or teachers, but we are all called to be "shepherds" of a few someday.

Share with your group what God is doing in your heart. God is searching for those whose hearts are fully his. Share your trials and victories. We promise that people will relate.

Prayerfully consider whom you would like to pass the baton to next week. It's only fair. God is ready for the next member of your group to go on the faith journey you just traveled. Make it fun, and expect God to do the rest.

LEADER'S NOTES

INTRODUCTION

Congratulations! You have responded to the call to help shepherd Jesus's flock. There are few other tasks in the family of God that surpass the contribution you will be making. We have provided you several ways to prepare for this role. Between the *Read Me First*, these *Leader's Notes*, and the *Watch This First* and *Leader Lifter* segments on the optional *Deepening Life Together: Ephesians* Video Teaching DVD, you'll have all you need to do a great job of leading your group. Just don't forget, you are not alone. God knew that you would be asked to lead this group and he won't let you down. In Hebrews 13:5b God promises us, "Never will I leave you; never will I forsake you" (NIV).

Your role as leader is to create a safe, warm environment for your group. As a leader, your most important job is to create an atmosphere where people are willing to talk honestly about what the topics discussed in this study have to do with them. Be available before people arrive so you can greet them at the door. People are naturally nervous at a new group, so a hug or handshake can help put them at ease. Before you start leading your group, a little preparation will give you confidence. Review the *Read Me First* at the front of your study guide so you'll understand the purpose of each section, enabling you to help your group understand it as well.

If you're new to leading a group, congratulations and thank you; this will be a life-changing experience for you also. We have provided these *Leader's Notes* to help new leaders begin well.

It's important in your first meeting to make sure group members understand that things shared personally and in prayer must remain confidential. Also, be careful not to dominate the group discussion, but facilitate it and encourage others to join in and share. And lastly, have fun.

Take a moment at the beginning of your first meeting to orient the group to one principle that undergirds this study: A healthy small group balances the purposes of the church. Most small groups emphasize Bible study, fellowship, and prayer. But God has called us to reach out to others as well. He wants us to do what Jesus teaches, not just learn about it.

Preparing for each meeting ahead of time. Take the time to review the session, the *Leader's Notes*, and *Leader Lifter* for the session before each session. Also write down your answers to each question. Pay special attention to exercises that ask group members to *do* something. These exercises will help your group live out what the Bible teaches, not just talk about it. Be sure you understand how the exercises work, and bring any supplies you might need, such as paper or pens. Pray for your group members by name at least once between sessions and before each session. Use the *Prayer and Praise Report* so you will remember their prayer requests. Ask God to use your time together to touch the heart of every person. Expect God to give you the opportunity to talk with those he wants you to encourage or challenge in a special way.

Don't try to go it alone. Pray for God to help you. Ask other members of your group to help by taking on some small role. In the *Appendix* you'll find the *Team Roles* pages with some suggestions to get people involved. Leading is more rewarding if you give group members opportunities to help. Besides, helping group members discover their individual gifts for serving or even leading the group will bless all of you.

Consider asking a few people to come early to help set up, pray, and introduce newcomers to others. Even if everyone is new, they don't know that yet and may be shy when they arrive. You might give people roles like setting up name tags or handing out drinks. This could be a great way to spot a co-leader.

Subgrouping. If your group has more than seven people, break into discussion groups of three to four people for the *Growing* and *Surrendering* sections each week. People will connect more with the study and each other when they have more opportunity to participate. Smaller discussion circles encourage quieter people to talk more and tend to minimize the effects of more vocal or dominant members. Also, people who are unaccustomed to praying aloud will feel more comfortable praying within a smaller group of people. Share prayer requests in the larger group and then break into smaller groups to pray for each other. People are more willing to pray in small circles if they know that the whole group will hear all the prayer requests.

Memorizing Scripture. At the start of each session you will find a memory verse—a verse for the group to memorize each week. Encourage your group members to do this. Memorizing God's Word is both directed and celebrated throughout the Bible, either explicitly ("Your word I have hidden in my heart, that I might not sin against You" [Ps. 119:11 NKJV]), or implicitly, as in the example of our Lord ("He departed to the mountain to pray" [Mark 6:46 NKJV]).

Anyone who has memorized Scripture can confirm the amazing spiritual benefits that result from this practice. Don't miss out on the opportunity to encourage your group to grow in the knowledge of God's Word through Scripture memorization.

Reflections. We've provided opportunity for a personal time with God using the *Reflections* at the end of each session. Don't press seekers to do this, but just remind the group that every believer should have a plan for personal time with God.

Inviting New People. Cast the vision, as Jesus did, to be inclusive not exclusive. Ask everyone to prayerfully think of people who would enjoy or benefit from a group like this—then invite them. The beginning of a new study is a great time to welcome a few people into your circle. Don't worry about ending up with too many people—you can always have one discussion circle in the living room and another in the dining room.

For Deeper Study (Optional). We have included a *For Deeper Study* section in each session. *For Deeper Study* provides additional passages for individual study on the topic of each session. If your group likes to do deeper Bible study, consider having members study the *For Deeper Study* passages for homework. Then, during the *Growing* portion of your meeting, you can share the high points of what you've learned.

LEADER'S NOTES
SESSIONS

Session One An Almighty God, a Glorious Church

Connecting

1. We've designed this study for both new and established groups, and for both seekers and the spiritually mature. New groups will need to invest more time building relationships with each other. Established groups often want to dig deeper into Bible study and application. Regardless of whether your group is new or has been together for a while, be sure to answer this introductory question at this first session.

2. A very important item in this first session is the *Small Group Agreement*. An agreement helps clarify your group's priorities and cast new vision for what the group can become. You can find this in the *Appendix*. We've found that groups that talk about these values up front and commit to an agreement benefit significantly. They work through conflicts long before people get to the point of frustration, so there's a lot less pain.

   Take some time to review this agreement before your meeting. Then during your meeting, read the agreement aloud to the entire group. If some people have concerns about a specific item or the agreement as a whole, be sensitive to their concerns. Explain that tens of thousands of groups use agreements like this one as a simple tool for building trust and group health over time.

   As part of this discussion, we recommend talking about shared ownership of the group. It's important that each member have a role. See the *Appendix* to learn more about *Team Roles*. This is a great tool to get this important practice launched in your group.

3. Note that this is a "what do you think" question. As such, there is no right or wrong answer. This question is intended to focus the group on the idea

that God does have a purpose and power in our lives that we will discover as we study the book of Ephesians together.

Growing

Have someone read Bible passages aloud. It's a good idea to ask ahead of time, because not everyone is comfortable reading aloud in public.

This session covers all of Ephesians chapter 1. Reading the entire selection aloud may be time-consuming so we recommend that you ask the group to read these passages at home before coming to the group.

4. Paul probably wants his readers to think about who they are, their identity as believers. They should think of themselves as "holy," set apart for God's purpose. He'll discuss faith/faithfulness later in this book, and he'll use the phrase "in Christ Jesus" over and over. The words "in Ephesus" are not present in the three earliest manuscripts. Therefore, this was very likely a circular letter, meaning the name of each local church would be filled in as the letter circulated from church to church. We can also learn some things about Paul from this greeting: he is an apostle and has a calling from God.

6. *God chose* (past tense) us out for himself—namely, *out of* the world (see Gal. 1:4). That God chose us forms the basis of the doctrine of election (see the *Study Notes* in this session for more information). God does not save us because we deserve it, but because he graciously and freely gives salvation according to his plan. We did not influence God's decision to save us; thus, we cannot take credit for our salvation. God's purpose in choosing us was so that we would live changed lives henceforth. To be "holy" means to be set apart for God in order to reflect his nature.

7. "Through his [Christ's] blood" is the key phrase. You could talk at length about how Christ's death buys you out of sin and death. Romans 10:9–10 (NIV) says "that if you confess with your mouth, 'Jesus is Lord,' and believe in your heart that God raised him from the dead, you will be saved. For it is with your heart that you believe and are justified, and it is with your mouth that you confess and are saved." When we do this, an exchange takes place. We give Christ our sins, and he gives us freedom and forgiveness—redemption.

8. God's kindness is showered on believers abundantly and extravagantly—lavishly. The mystery is God's revealed plan to bring people, both Jews and Gentiles, back into fellowship with himself through their faith in Christ and then to keep them with him for all eternity.

9. God reveals himself to his people through the presence of the Holy Spirit in their lives. The Holy Spirit fills us with a sense of God's love (Rom. 5:5),

assures us that God has adopted us as his children (Rom. 8:15–16), and helps us to demonstrate Christ through out lives. The Holy Spirit is God's guarantee that he will give believers everything he promised. The Spirit is the first payment of all the treasures that will be ours because he has purchased us to be his own people. The presence of the Holy Spirit in us proves that we are God's children and secures eternal life for us. His power works in us to transform us now, and what we experience now is a taste of the total change we will experience in eternity.

10. Paul asked that God would give the Ephesian believers spiritual wisdom and understanding. Wisdom is the ability to see life from God's perspective—to have discernment. Understanding refers to an enlightened knowledge of God.

11. In the Bible the "heart" is the center of one's personhood or being. Paul prayed that the believers might have true spiritual insight into God. Spiritual enlightenment is necessary, because while the information about Christ is available to anyone who chooses to read the Bible, it doesn't fully sink in without God's help.

12. The power is available "for us who believe." Faith is necessary. Only God's power can change weak human beings into strong believers who are willing to sacrifice everything for the God who loves them. With the second part of this question, try to get practical. Consistent attention to the Holy Spirit is important for accessing his power.

Developing

This section enables you to help the group see the importance of developing their abilities for service to God.

13. The intent of this question is to encourage group members to set aside some time to spend with God in prayer and his Word at home each day throughout the week. Read through this section and be prepared to help the group understand how important it is to fill our minds with the Word of God. If people already have a good Bible reading plan and commitment, that is great, but you may have people who struggle to stay in the Word daily. Sometimes beginning with a simple commitment to a short daily reading can start a habit that changes a life. The *Reflections* pages at the end of each session include verses that were either talked about in the session or support the teaching of the session. They are very short readings with a few lines to encourage people to write down their thoughts. Remind the group about these *Reflections* each week after the *Surrendering* section. Encourage everyone to commit to a next step in prayer, Bible reading, or meditation on the Word.

Sharing

Jesus wants all of his disciples to help outsiders connect with him, to know him personally. This section should provide an opportunity to go beyond Bible study to biblical living.

14. Encourage the group to observe their interactions during the coming week with the intention of using these observations next week in evaluating the people that God has placed in their lives that he might want them to share with or invite to your small group.

Surrendering

16. Encourage group members to use the *Reflections* verses in their daily quiet time throughout the week. This will move them closer to God while reinforcing the lesson of this session through related Scripture.

17. As you move to a time of sharing prayer requests, be sure to remind the group of the importance of confidentiality and keeping what is shared in the group within the group. Everyone must feel that the personal things they share will be kept confident if you are to have safety and bonding among group members.

    Use the *Prayer and Praise Report* in the *Appendix* to record your prayer requests. There you can keep track of requests and celebrate answers to prayer.

Session Two Before and After Christ

Connecting

2. We encourage the group to rotate hosts/leaders and homes each meeting. This practice will go a long way toward bonding the group. Review the *Small Group Calendar* and talk about who else is willing to open their home or facilitate a meeting. Rotating host homes and leadership along with implementing *Team Roles* as discussed in *Session One* will quickly move the group ownership from "your group" to "our group."

Growing

This session covers all of Ephesians chapter 2. Reading the entire selection aloud may be time-consuming so we recommend that you ask the group to read these passages at home before coming to the group.

4. To be "dead in your transgressions (trespass) and sins" is to be spiritually dead, having no communication with God. One who is spiritually dead is not physically dead, but their sins have left them spiritually unresponsive, alienated from God, and consequently incapable of experiencing the full life that a relationship with God could give them.

   All of us were at one time separated from God because of the disobedience of Adam and Eve. We were born with a sinful nature. That nature puts us under God's anger. When we become believers, our sinful nature still exists. But when we submit our lives to Christ, the Holy Spirit transforms us and our sinful natures.

5. Being "alive in Christ" is the essential point of Ephesians. It means we have identified with Christ in his death and resurrection. We are risen again to new spiritual life—we are spiritually alive. Christ defeated sin and death through his death and resurrection, thus offering spiritual life to those dead in sins. God then gives us victory over sin through the Holy Spirit, who lives in us and gives us power to live as people "in Christ," increasingly free from sin's compulsion. To restrain the desires of the sinful nature, we must be willing to depend on God and his mercy.

6. From eternity, in his love, God chose us to be holy before him. Believers are examples of his favor and kindness, now and forever. When dead in trespasses and sins, he made us alive, raised us up, and made us to sit together in heavenly realms with Christ. Our salvation through Christ Jesus glorifies God for his endless grace and kindness. All of heaven glorifies him for what he has done for us.

7. Our salvation comes from God's special favor alone. We appropriate it when we believe. However, lest anyone should think that belief is a necessary work that must be performed in order to receive salvation, Paul adds that people can't take credit for believing, for it too is a gift from God. Paul is firm that absolutely nothing is of our own doing—not salvation, not grace, not even the faith exercised to receive salvation. Instead, everything is the gift of God. Salvation does not come from our self-reliance or individualism but from God's initiative. It is a gift to be thankfully accepted.

8. While no action or work we do can help us obtain salvation, God intends that our salvation will result in acts of service. People become Christians through God's undeserved favor (his grace), not as the result of any efforts, abilities, choices, characteristics, or acts of service. Out of gratitude for God's free gift of salvation, however, believers will want to do good things— to help and serve others. These are the "works" referred to in verse 10. In verse 9, works refers to the observance of the law of Moses.

9. God brought restoration for broken relationships through Christ, even reconciliation between Jews and Gentiles. It is only through Christ that the Gentiles could be joined with Jewish believers as part of the same church.

There should be no barriers, divisions, or discrimination. We all belong to Christ and share fully in his blessings.

10. Paul uses a metaphor to describe the church. Presumably, every well-built structure with a firm foundation has a cornerstone. God's house is built on a solid foundation—the apostles and the prophets—with Christ as the cornerstone. Each part of the building is a believer who fits perfectly into the building, all being aligned with the cornerstone. The structure is not yet complete; it will not be complete until the day that Christ Jesus returns. The building's purpose is to be a holy temple for the Lord, where God's presence is evident.

Developing

11. For many, spiritual partners will be a new idea. We highly encourage you to try pairs for this study. It's so hard to start a spiritual practice like prayer or consistent Bible reading with no support. A friend makes a huge difference. As leader, you may want to prayerfully decide who would be a good match with whom. Remind people that this partnership isn't forever; it's just for a few weeks. Be sure to have extra copies of the *Personal Health Plan* available at this meeting in case you need to have a group of three spiritual partners. It is a good idea for you to look over the *Personal Health Plan* before the meeting so you can help people understand how to use it.

   Instruct your group members to enlist a spiritual partner by asking them to pair up with someone in the group (we suggest that men partner with men and women with women) and turn to the *Personal Health Plan*.

   Ask the group to complete the instructions for the WHO and WHAT questions on the *Personal Health Plan*. Your group has now begun to address two of God's purposes for their lives!

   You can see that the *Personal Health Plan* contains space to record the ups and downs and progress each week in the column labeled "My Progress." When partners check in each week, they can record their partner's progress in the goal he or she chose in the "Partner's Progress" column on this chart. You'll find a *Sample Personal Health Plan* filled in as an example.

12. Encourage the group to plan a social or potluck outside of small group time. Socializing together provides the group an opportunity to build stronger relationships between individual members as well as allows time for celebrating what God is doing through this small group Bible study.

   The WHERE, WHEN, and HOW questions on the *Personal Health Plan* will be addressed in future sessions of the study.

Sharing

13. A *Circles of Life* diagram is provided for you and the group to use to help you identify people who need a connection to Christian community. Encourage the group to commit to praying for God's guidance and an opportunity to reach out to each person in their *Circles of Life*.

We encourage this outward focus for your group because groups that become too inwardly focused tend to become unhealthy over time. People naturally gravitate toward feeding themselves through Bible study, prayer, and social time, so it's usually up to the leader to push them to consider how this inward nourishment can overflow into outward concern for others. Never forget: Jesus came to seek and save the lost and to find a shepherd for every sheep.

Talk to the group about the importance of inviting people; remind them that healthy small groups make a habit of inviting friends, neighbors, unconnected church members, co-workers, etc., to join their groups or join them at a weekend church service. When people get connected to a group of new friends, they often join the church.

Some groups are happy with the people they already have in the group and they don't really want to grow larger. Some fear that newcomers will interrupt the intimacy that members have built over time. However, groups generally gain strength with the infusion of new people. It's like a river of living water flowing into a stagnant pond. Some groups remain permanently open, while others open periodically, such as at the beginning and end of a study. If your circle becomes too large for easy face-to-face conversations, you can simply form a second or third discussion circle in another room in your home.

Surrendering

15. Last week we talked briefly about incorporating *Reflections* into the group members' daily time with God. Some people don't yet have an established quiet time. With this in mind, engage a discussion within the group about the importance of making daily time with God a priority. Talk about potential obstacles and practical ideas for how to overcome them. The *Reflections* verses could serve as a springboard for drawing near to God. So don't forget these are a valuable resource for your group.

16. Be sure to remind the group of the importance of confidentiality and keeping what is shared in the group within the group. Use the *Prayer and Praise Report* in the *Appendix* to record your prayer requests.

Session Three God's Mystery Revealed

Connecting

1. Encourage group members to take time to complete the *Personal Health Assessment* and pair up with their spiritual partner to discuss one thing that is going well and one thing that needs work. Participants should not be asked to share any aspect of this assessment in the large group if they don't want to.

Growing

This session covers all of Ephesians chapter 3. Reading the entire selection aloud may be time-consuming so we recommend that you ask the group to read these passages at home before coming to the group.

3. Paul indicates that he received the mystery referred to in verse 3 in a revelation from God. This was in a direct communication from God to Ananias (Acts 9:15). This wasn't something Paul thought up on his own. He claims the authority of an apostle.

4. God revealed to Paul that Jesus Christ truly was the promised Messiah of the Jews and the light to the Gentiles too. Both Jews and Gentiles would be included in the church. All mankind is united into one under Christ.

5. Paul was raised as a faithful and devoted Jew, and trained by Gamaliel, one of the leading rabbis of his day. Before becoming a Christian, he had persecuted the church, believing that Jesus was a false Messiah and that the Christians were heretics. Paul is overwhelmed that, despite this past, God had chosen him and saved him for the purpose of telling the Gentiles about Christ.

6. Paul describes the believer's ability to come fearlessly into God's presence as the most awesome privilege anyone could have. Because of this—his own awesome privilege—he does not want readers to despair over his suffering through imprisonment. Paul considers it a privilege to suffer for championing the ministry of the gospel to the Gentiles (thus bringing others to the freedom and confidence he enjoys), and he encourages believers to consider it an honor too.

7. "That Christ may dwell in your hearts through faith" (v. 17a). Christ dwelling in believers' hearts conveys the idea of settling down, taking up permanent residence. The "heart" in the Bible always refers to the center of a person's emotions and will. Christ takes up permanent residence in the hearts of those who trust in him, changing their "heart" and, consequently, their words and thoughts.

9. The ultimate goal of our existence is to bring glory to God.

Developing

10. The group members should consider where they can take a next step toward getting involved in ministering to the body of Christ in your local church. Discuss some of the ministries that your church may offer to people looking to get involved such as the children's ministry, ushering, or hospitality. Remind everyone that it sometimes takes time and trying several different ministries before finding the one that fits best.

11. Encourage group members to use the *Personal Health Plan* to jot down their next step to serving in ministry, with a plan for how and when they will begin.

Sharing

12. It is important to return to the *Circles of Life* and encourage the group to follow through on their commitments to invite people who need to know Christ more deeply through Christian community. When people are asked why they never go to church, they often say, "No one ever invited me." Remind the group that our responsibility is to invite people, but it is the Holy Spirit's responsibiliy to compel them to come.

Session Four Empowered to Live and Serve

Growing

This session covers all of Ephesians chapter 4. Reading the entire selection aloud may be time-consuming so we recommend that you ask the group to read these passages at home before coming to the group.

4. "It was he who gave some to be apostles, some to be prophets, some to be evangelists, and some to be pastors and teachers" (Eph. 4:11 NIV). The gifts are leaders, and they are given for the equipping of God's people.

     Immature Christians are easily led astray. The job of leaders is not to do all the work in the church, but to equip the less mature for works of service so that they won't be led astray. Of course, believers have to want to be equipped for service.

5. "Futility" in verse 17 means worthlessness or meaninglessness. Futile thinking is aiming at pointless goals with worthless methods. How meaningful are your goals? How worthwhile are your methods for pursuing them?

6. Believers are told to "put off" their old self. This means to stop living according to the habits of their sinful nature and to be made new by the power of the Holy Spirit. This entails a spiritual renewal of our thoughts and attitudes (v. 23). As long as we live on this earth, we will struggle with

this, but we need to devote energy to cooperating with the Holy Spirit on the transformation of our thinking.

Developing

9. Point the group to the *Spiritual Gifts Inventory* in the *Appendix*. Read through the spiritual gifts and engage the group in discussion about which gifts they believe they have. Encourage group members to review these further on their own time during the coming week, giving prayerful consideration to each one. We will refer back to this again later in the study.

10. It's time to start thinking about what your group will do when you're finished with this study. Now is the time to ask how many people will be joining you so you can choose a study and have the books available when you meet for the final session of this study.

Sharing

11. This activity provides an opportunity for the group to share Jesus in a very practical way. Discuss this and choose one action step to take as a group. Be certain that everyone understands his or her role in this activity. It might be a good idea to call each person before the next meeting to remind people to bring to the next session what is required of them.

   Designate one person to investigate where to donate items in your area. That person can also be responsible for dropping off the items.

12. Encourage group members to think about when they are shepherding another person in Christ. This could be simply following through on inviting someone to church or reaching out to them in Christ's love. Then have everyone answer the question "WHEN are you shepherding another person in Christ?" on the *Personal Health Plan*.

Session Five Living Responsibly

Growing

This session covers Ephesians 5:1–6:9. Reading the entire selection aloud may be time-consuming so we recommend that you ask the group to read these passages at home before coming to the group.

3. We are to follow the example of God's great love for us that led him to sacrifice his Son so that we might live. We can do that by living a life filled with love for others.

5. A life redeemed (by the blood of Christ) and brought into the light (his truth) must not continue in the darkness of a sinful lifestyle. Salvation is by grace, not works, but it's inconceivable to Paul that a saved person will continue living like an unsaved one.

7. Believers are to make the most of the brief time God has given them on this evil earth—filling our time with activities that fulfill God's purposes. Every opportunity should be spent in worship and service to Christ's church.

8. Ephesians 5:19–21 says, "Speak to one another with psalms, hymns and spiritual songs. Sing and make music in your heart to the Lord, always giving thanks to God the Father for everything, in the name of our Lord Jesus Christ" (NIV). Spirit-filled worship, sung together in praise to God, is evidence of the Holy Spirit's presence.

9. Mutual submission preserves order and harmony. Submission is evidence that we have Spirit-controlled relationships. This requires the Holy Spirit's guidance and restraint (4:2–3).

10. The home, the foundation for relationships and personal growth, is used as an example of what submission should be—giving yourself for the good of others. In a marriage relationship, both husband and wife are called to submit. The relationship between spouses represents the larger picture of church relationships. Submission can only be offered, extended, offered freely—it cannot be demanded. Jesus modeled ultimate submission on the cross.

    The wife's submission to her husband is one way that she can demonstrate her submission to Christ. She does this voluntarily out of love for her husband and for Christ.

    Here marriage is a picture of the relationship between Christ and his church. Husbands are called to love their wives with the same love Christ showed the church. That Christ gave up his life for the church indicates a sacrificial, substitutionary surrender of himself to death. Christ sacrificed himself for the church because of his love for it. Husbands, then, should be ready to do likewise, often sacrificing their desires for the good of their wives. Marriage is a holy union, a living symbol, a precious relationship that needs tender, self-sacrificing care.

11. Although submission to parents should be for the Lord's sake, God has graciously added the promise of special blessing for those who obey the command to honor their parents. As we obey the command to honor our parents, we show an attitude of love and respect that we carry over into our relationship with God.

    To obey means to do what another says to do; to honor means to respect and love.

Developing

13. If members of the group have committed to spending time alone with God, congratulate them and encourage them to take their commitment one step further and begin journaling. Review *Journaling 101* in the *Appendix* prior to your group time so that you are familiar with what it contains.

Sharing

15. It is important to return to the *Circles of Life* often, both to encourage the group to follow through on their commitments as well as to foster growth toward new commitments. Encourage the group this week to consider reaching out to their non-Christian friends, family, and acquaintances. Remind everyone that our responsibility is to share Jesus with others, but it is the Holy Spirit's responsibility to convict souls and bring forth change.

16. Discuss the implication of Jesus's mandate to take the gospel to the "ends of the earth" on the lives of believers today. Have each person consider the action steps listed and choose one to begin immediately as a way of doing their part in seeing this accomplished.

Surrendering

18. Have everyone answer the question "HOW are you surrendering your heart?" on the *Personal Health Plan.*

Session Six Waging Spiritual Warfare

Connecting

2. Take a few minutes for group members to share one thing they learned or a commitment they made or renewed during this study. They may also want to share what they enjoyed most about the study and about this group.

    Be prepared to offer some suggested resources for answering questions that may arise from this study. Offer other Scripture that relates to the topics studied. Ask your pastor to suggest some helpful books or articles. Advise group members to schedule a meeting with a pastor to get answers to difficult questions. Whatever you do, don't let anyone leave with unanswered questions or without the resources to find the answers they seek.

Growing

This session covers Ephesians 6:10–6:20. Ask the group to read these passages at home before coming to the group.

3. Our spiritual struggle is against the devil's schemes—against the rulers and authorities and powers of this dark world and the spiritual forces of evil in the heavenly realms. Human effort is inadequate against them; verse 10 indicates that we need the Lord's mighty power to stand against them. The believer's role is to draw strength from the Lord and then take a stand against the devil's schemes.

7. Praying in the Spirit means that we live in dependence on God's Spirit and that the Spirit helps us when we pray. The Spirit prays on our behalf, makes God accessible, gives us confidence, and inspires and guides us when we pray. (See also Rom. 8:15–16, 26–27; Eph. 2:18; and Gal. 4:6.)

8. Paul does not pray for his personal well-being; he asks believers to pray that he would have boldness and faithfulness needed to continue preaching the gospel—to persevere in the work that God gave him to do. God's kingdom can benefit from believers praying this for each other as well.

Developing

9. This activity provides an opportunity for the group to share Jesus in a very practical way. Discuss this with the group and choose one action step to take as a group. Invite one person to volunteer to be the point person on this. They would investigate the action step you have chosen and report back to the group what they find out. For example, if you have chosen to do yard work, the point person would contact the church to find a needy family and schedule the work to be done. It is ideal that every member of the group participates, but don't wait until all schedules align before making a plan to follow through. Many times, waiting until eight or ten individuals are available can cause a plan to fizzle out entirely.

10. If you haven't already done so, you'll want to take time to finalize plans for the future of your group. You need to talk about whether you will continue together as a group, who will lead, and where you will meet.
   As you discuss the future of your group, talk about how well you achieved the goals you made in the *Small Group Agreement*. Address any changes you'd like to make as you move forward.

Sharing

11. Allow one or two group members to share for a few minutes a testimony about how they helped someone connect in Christian community or shared Jesus with an unbelieving friend or relative.

12. Understanding the Holy Spirit's role in revealing spiritual truth to unbelievers can relieve any burden or need we may feel to be sure they understand our message. Our responsibility is to share truth, not to make people understand it. The Holy Spirit continues to work in the life of the unbeliever long after we have gone.

    Understanding this should encourage believers to share the truth because we can know that not only our words are Spirit empowered, but the strength with which we speak is from the Spirit as well. The message is not our own, but the Spirit's, and we are not alone in sharing.

13. Encourage group members to consider developing their salvation story as a tool for sharing their faith with others. Begin the process during your group time and encourage the group to complete the exercise at home. As leader, you should review the Tips section of *Telling Your Story* yourself in advance and be ready to share your ideas about this process with the group.

DEEPENING LIFE TOGETHER SERIES

Deepening Life Together is a series of Bible studies that offers small groups an opportunity to explore biblical subjects in several categories: books of the Bible (*Acts, Romans, John, Ephesians, Revelation*), theology (*Promises of God, Parables*), and spiritual disciplines (*Prayers of Jesus*).

A *Deepening Life Together* Video Teaching DVD companion is available for each study in the series. For each study session, the DVD contains a lesson taught by a master teacher backed by scholars giving their perspective on the subject.

Every study includes activities based on five biblical purposes of the church: Connecting, Growing, Developing, Sharing, and Surrendering. These studies will help your group deepen your walk with God while you discover what he has created you for and how you can turn his desires into an everyday reality in your lives. Experience the transformation firsthand as you begin deepening your life together.